03/10/2019

mane

MW00771976

PLENITUDE

DIVALDO FRANCO
BY THE SPIRIT JOANNA DE ÂNGELIS

PLENITUDE

LEAL Publisher

Copyright© 2016 by
Centro Espírita Caminho da Redenção – Salvador (BA) – Brazil

All rights reserved. No part of this book may be reproduced by any mechanical, photographic, or electronic process, or in the form of a phonographic recording; nor may it be stored in a retrieval system, transmitted, or otherwise be copied for public or private use without prior written permission of the publisher.

ISBN: 978-1-942408-51-2

Original title in Portuguese:
Plenitude
(Brazil, 1991)

Translated by: Darrel W. Kimble and Claudia Dealmeida
Cover design by: Cláudio Urpia
Layout: Luciano Carneiro Holanda
Edited by: Evelyn Yuri Furuta

Edition of
LEAL PUBLISHER
8425 Biscayne Blvd. Suite 104
Miami, Florida 33138, USA
www.lealpublisher.com
info@lealpublisher.com
(305) 306-6447

Authorized edition by Centro Espírita Caminho da Redenção – Salvador (BA) – Brazil

INTERNATIONAL DATA FOR CATALOGING IN PUBLICATION (ICP)

f825   Ângelis, de Joanna (Spirit).
          Plenitude / authored by the Spirit Joanna de Ângelis;
          psychographed by Divaldo Pereira Franco ; translated by Darrel Kimble and
          Claudia Dealmeida. – Miami (FL), USA : Leal Publisher, 2016.

          147 p. ; 21 cm

          Original title: Plenitude

          ISBN 978-1-942408-51-2

          1. Spiritism. 2. Psychology. 3. Feelings
          I. Franco, Divaldo Pereira, 1927-. II. Title.
                                              CDD 133.9
                                              CDU 133.7

CONTENTS

PLENITUDE[1]

*P*essimistic philosophies and arbitrary religious doctrines have established that life means suffering, and therefore every attempt at release from suffering results in failure.

Faithful to this ignoble diagnosis, rash thinkers of yesterday and today have proposed suicide, euthanasia and abortion as escape mechanisms for dealing with distressing situations, and the death penalty as a means of punishment. All these approaches are the result of merciless and rebellious materialistic behavior, where cruelty assumes the leading role.

Such individuals build their aspirations on utilitarianism and hedonism, but these are responsible for the distorted view of reality, from which they wish to be free.

---

[1] Plenitude or the *numinous** is the hidden treasure within the depths of the Self, which everyone must achieve by absorbing the shadow and sublimating the perturbing archetypes. This results in a state of inner harmony that provides a cosmic view of life into which the Self must integrate. *Espelhos da Alma* [Mirrors of the Soul], Third Part, pp. 239-241, Joanna de Ângelis, LEAL (1st. Ed. – 2015). – Tr.

* *Numinous*: A neologism coined in 1917 by a German professor of theology, Rudolf Otto. In Otto's and Jung's usage, "spiritual," "holy," "divine," and "intangible" capture most accurately the qualities they mean. http://jungiancenter.org – Tr.

Of course, suffering is part of life. It is nature's device, through which intellectual and moral progress is expressed and consolidated.

The diamond in the rough waits to be polished in order to shine like a luminous star.

Metals require high temperatures in order to be shaped for beauty and usefulness.

Wood endures cutting tools so that it can fulfill the important roles for which it is intended.

The river carves out its own bed.

Likewise, the spirit needs to polish the edges that hide its light, and for that reason suffering is a normal occurrence, which knowledge and willpower can direct in a balanced way so that suffering can fulfill its sublime purpose.

On the other hand, suffering is linked to each person's sensitivity; thus, it varies and takes on different dimensions accordingly. The pain of the brute is wild and perturbing, exploding in aggression and madness, whereas the suffering of the esthete and the saint is expressed as a yearning for deliverance and inner growth.

As it goes through the first stages of life, thanks to its evolutionary automatisms, the psyche expands its innate aptitudes and develops its dormant seeds of perfection, becoming heir to its past experiences.

Because suffering entails bitterness and pain, it has warranted the broadest historical investment ever heard of, aiming at deliverance from it on the one hand, and the plenitude of the individual on the other.

From Krishna to Buddha, to Jesus, to Allan Kardec,[2] religious and philosophical insight into suffering has received

---

[2] Allan Kardec (1804-1869), Codifier of Spiritism – Tr.

8

invaluable contributions that today, with the efforts of modern, holistic health scientists, seem to have arrived at a greater understanding of human beings and their inter-relationship with the living forces of nature, reflected in ecology. This has allowed for a greater understanding of life and its purpose.

Anticipating such modern-day behavior, Spiritism has been summoning human beings to respect God, themselves, each other, and all living and non-living expressions that comprise their environment, in order to learn and be happy, thus acquiring plenitude.

Considering the human quandary individuals are faced with – their lack of self-knowledge – and considering the pressing factors that trigger suffering, dragging multitudes into folly, despair, insanity and shameful escape by means of suicide and vice, we decided to delve into studies about suffering, and we offer them to the esteemed reader interested in solving this terrible scourge responsible for countless ills for some and blessings for others, enabling the latter to ascend and to succeed...

We analyze some of the aspects of suffering from the Buddhist and Christian perspectives, and propose the Spiritist solution due to the timeliness of the postulates that comprise the Revelation of the Consoler, inviting humans to self-discovery, to living the Gospel, and to the lucid behavior resulting from study and illuminative work on the path of fraternal charity.

We trust that our effort will contribute to the enlightenment of our readers, inducing them to acquire plenitude, in peace and health, entirely free of suffering, constructing love as a living fount of inner and common realization.

*In hopes of having achieved our goal, we pray to Jesus –
Humanity's Model and Guide – to bless and guide us.*

JOANNA DE ÂNGELIS
Salvador, Brazil, October 17, 1990

O Lord!
Help me to cross: from darkness to the light; from
falsehood to truth; and from death to immortality.
Upanishads

Sit alone and in silence.
Bow your head and close your eyes; relax your
breathing and with your imagination look into your
heart; direct your thoughts from your head to your
heart.
And while exhaling say "Lord Jesus Christ, have
mercy on me."

Gregory of Sinai – Monastery of Mt. Athos – 14th Century

1
SUFFERING

Humans strive laboriously to overcome suffering, which they see as a vile enemy.

Throughout history they have waged an ongoing, fierce but unsuccessful battle to evade pain, exhausting their strength, courage and balance, only to fall into even worse afflictions afterwards.

To get through suffering unscathed is everyone's main goal, or at least to relieve it somewhat in order to enjoy the endless varieties of the pleasures of life.

Desirous of instant gratification, they are interested only in today and have no vision of the future.

Consequently, suffering has been seen as divine punishment or revenge, and thus an object of abhorrence and hatred.

In various mythologies, the figures of jealous, spiteful gods inflicting punishment on people and taking pleasure in their pain have been the age-old answer to earthly suffering.

The different philosophical schools and religious doctrines somewhat in agreement with such an absurd notion have established purifying methods for release from suffering. These methods range from the most barbaric scourges – cilices, ritual killings, promises and offerings – to the severest asceticism, seeking to *deny the world and hate it* so that, by assuming such postures, they might *pacify and please the gods or God.*

At the same time, stoicism, heir to certain Eastern behaviors, has attempted to immunize people against suffering by encouraging them to lead lives of serious sacrifice – in itself a cause of suffering.

To break free of this *foe*, people impose on themselves other forms of pain, which they accept rationally and freely, not realizing their mistaken notion.

Pain, however, is not a punishment. Instead, it is one of life's excellent devices for achieving its own goals.

A phenomenon of wear and tear due to natural alterations in the structure of the organs – as the consumption of energy leads to the deterioration of the material envelope that it vitalizes – this disjunction is accompanied by the unpleasant sensations of anguish, pain and imbalance, depending on the individual's affected area.

Thus, human suffering on the earth, as well as in the vibratory areas that surround it, is unavoidable. Suffering is part of the evolutionary stage of the planet and of all its inhabitants as they make their way to higher planes.

Since suffering has a variety of causes, every effort to mitigate it without removing them will work only as a palliative and postponement. Even when a form of treatment does reward patients with sudden release, if the treatment did not reach the causes that triggered the suffering, they will go from one problem to the next without having acquired real health.

This is because in every degenerative process or affliction, the spirit itself is always responsible, consciously or not. And of course, peace arises only once the spirit has chosen inner harmony.

In such a situation, even in the event of biological changes, the ensuing suffering does not affect the emotions or become harmful. Like other physiological automatisms, the conscience simply does not register its manifestation.

Suffering, therefore, can and should be considered a *disease of the soul,* which still clings to sensations favoring paths and actions that produce imbalance. During this immediate interest phase, a whole tangle of primitive passions drives individuals devoid of the necessary ethics or proper discriminating sense to seek pleasure. Consequently, they get entangled in conflicts that break down the body's defenses, which yield to insatiable, devouring, invading, immunity-destroying microbes and viruses.

Likewise, the ultrasensitive mental component is thrown into disarray, opening the way to insanity and cruel obsessions.[3]

By extension, one has to say that suffering is not imposed by God; instead, people choose it themselves, for its intensity and duration are in direct proportion to individuals' evolutionary structure and the moral resistance characteristic of their spiritual level.

Emotional sensitivity is what filters and externalizes pain. When there is little sensitivity, aggressions of all kinds are met with violence and hostility.

On the more primitive evolutionary levels, since *beings* are almost destitute of reasoning and emotion – which are still in seed form – the phenomena of pain, decay, aging

---

[3] The domination that some spirits acquire over certain people. For more in-depth information please refer to chapter XXIII of *The Medium's Book* by Allan Kardec – Tr.

and death follow an automatist, directional course, in which exceptions attest to the journey of the *conscious essence* to higher levels.

Thus, suffering is greatest in the mental and emotional realms, which are only found in bearers of a higher degree of evolution, sensitivity and love, those who can use self-control to overcome such afflicting conditions with hope, tenderness and the certainty of victory.

Fleeing, hiding and anesthetizing suffering are ineffective. They are only mechanisms of escape that postpone reality, further adding to the already existing overload of complications resulting from wasted time. On the other hand, courageously examining and facing it is a valuable and lucid resource that has the therapeutic effect of bringing peace.

Reactions of anger, violence and rebelliousness only increase suffering by triggering further disharmony in previously unaffected areas.

Dynamic resignation, that is, accepting the problem with the courage to face and remove its cause, is a major step toward solving it.

Mental and moral balance in the face of suffering is of unsuspected, positive value, and can be achieved through the practice of meditation and prayer, which derive from the knowledge that illuminates and properly guides the conscience.

The awareness that one is an immortal spirit evolving by means of successive reincarnations represents a major acquisition for understanding, considering and overcoming suffering, which is part of the *modus operandi* of all beings.

Many people argue that suffering is life's only certainty, but they do not understand that it is in direct proportion to each individual's past or present conduct.

One can therefore say that suffering results from distancing oneself from love, which is its best and most effective antidote.

Suffering and love are evolution's interdependent driving forces. When one recedes, the other comes forth. Sometimes, crowning the final step of the struggle, they occur simultaneously but without the harm that they normally cause.

The story of the martyrs attests to the veracity of this concept.

Above them all, however, the example of Jesus stands out. Through love, Jesus taught victory over suffering throughout His entire life, especially in the climactic moments from Gethsemane to Golgotha, and from there to resurrection...

The phenomena of life may be likened unto a dream, a phantasm, a bubble, a shadow, the glistening dew, or lightening flash; and thus they ought to be contemplated.

The Buddha — *The Immutable Sutra*

2
AN ANALYSIS
OF SUFFERING

The Buddha taught that life's only purpose is the struggle for victory over suffering. Striving to overcome it must be one's constant concern.

After attempting to overcome suffering by means of the most austere asceticism and strictest discipline, the young Gautama left the monastery with a few discouraged followers and began meditating calmly, achieving Enlightenment.

He established the theory of the "middle way" to find peace: neither cruel austerity nor the usual self-indulgence, but the balance of meditation.

He then turned his attention to individuals' liberation and established the four *Noble Truths: suffering, its origins, the end of suffering, and the paths to liberation from suffering.*

According to his way of thinking, *suffering* appears in three different forms: *suffering from suffering, suffering from impermanence, and suffering resulting from conditionings.*

Suffering from suffering is the result of afflictions caused by suffering per se.

Suffering tortures the sentiments, disheartens fragile psychological structures, causes unhappiness, leads to erroneous conclusions and stimulates the states of emotional elation or depression, depending on the individual's inner composition.

In the vast area of pathologies, suffering presents itself under two aspects: *physical and mental.* In this case, *suffering is like an illness* that is both cause and effect.

Illnesses, however, are inevitable during the physical existence due to the body's molecular composition and the biological phenomena to which it is subjected in its unceasing transformations.

The scope of the action of matter upon the spirit, particularly in the earliest stages, entails constant suffering due to continuous physical illnesses and frequent mental dystonia.

Like the chisel shaping the rough stone, illnesses are mechanisms for the soul to awaken to its abilities and shine beyond the organic vessel imprisoning it.

Medical science has achieved a high level of knowledge in this area, and has cured age-old diseases that used to decimate millions of lives, creating mass hysteria.

Clarity of diagnosis, surgical skill, a wide range of pharmaceuticals, and various alternative therapies have all contributed a large contingent of aid to attend to the sick. In spite of periodic outbreaks of age-old ills and the emergence of others caused by improvidence, this significant achievement has done much to relieve suffering.

In the area of psychopathology, the human perspective is now more benign than in the past. Mentally ill persons are seen as human beings, who, although having momentarily lost their îdentity and balance, have the right to assistance, opportunity and love.

Unfortunately, however, existential and behavioral disturbances have multiplied in the psychological arena, giving rise to the so-called *neurotic generation* lost in the *mare magnum* as victims of misguided sex, addictive drugs, urban violence, and defiant cynicism.

Technological advances have not blocked the conduits of despair; today's hedonistic culture, which is indifferent toward moral values, and continuous wars have fomented fear, dissatisfaction, desperation and emotional escapes.

Insecure youth have become despair's biggest victims, and are one step away from depression, madness and suicide.

Alongside today's diverse and desperate pathologies, the psychological phenomena of imbalance have spread out of control.

The human mass has begun to suffer the effects of this widespread suffering.

Illness, however, is the result of an imbalance in the energies of the body due to the emotional fragility of the spirit acting upon it. Viruses, bacteria and other destructive microorganisms are not actually responsible for illness. Instead, the cells nourish them as they begin inhabiting the areas where the energy has waned. They cause physical and mental weakness, which fosters the emergence of illness due to the depletion of health-sustaining energy. Drugs may kill these *invaders*, but they do not restore the desired balance if the preserving *source* does not emit the force that sustains the body.

With the death of the microbes, the patient seems to have recovered. But it is only temporary, because the situation will resurface later as another pathology.

When people's mental and moral conduct cultivates irritability, hatred, jealousy, rancor or wastefulness, it impregnates the nervous system with deleterious vibrations that block the areas through which healthy energy travels, making way for the onset of illnesses due to the proliferation of the degenerative viral agents settling there.

Traditional therapies nearly always remove the symptoms but do not reach the root causes of illnesses.

Healing always comes from the power of life itself, when such power is properly channeled.

Physical, mental and emotional forms of stress are also responsible for illnesses – *suffering, which begets suffering.*

Ever since their social origins, people have learned to be afraid, to hold on to anger, to be thrown off by minor events, thus disarticulating their energy system. They go from one annoyance to another, cultivating *emotional viruses* that promote the installation of degenerative viruses that make their illnesses even worse.

Conditionings, pessimistic ideas, preposterous beliefs and aggravations are responsible for the tensions leading to disharmony.

When individuals avoid such burdens, their *energetic-immunological* system will free them from their illnesses and their lives will change, thus improving their health.

The root causes of illnesses, therefore, lie within individuals themselves, who must engage in self-examination in order to be released from this kind of suffering.

There is also *pleasure that begets suffering.*

Everyday life shows that the insatiable pursuit of pleasure is a torment that afflicts without reward. When one does get the opportunity to enjoy it, it is obvious that the price was too high and the resultant sensation was not worth it.

Moreover, there are acquisitions that provide pleasure at one moment but soon turn into bitter pain. Illusion is responsible for this. Most suffering arises from the mistaken way one looks at life. Because life is transitory, real values transcend the forms and motivations that generate pleasure.

This is *suffering from the impermanence* of earthly things. They vanish like chaff in a fire fanned by the wind, and soon become ash floating in the air.

To actually enjoy a certain pleasure, individuals invest in it beyond their possibilities, only to realize afterwards how hard it is to hold on to the object of their desire. The struggle to own the latest model of car exposes them to heavy debt in the future. Their imagination stimulates them with the illusion of ownership, but once the pleasure fades away, they find that they cannot afford to maintain the vehicle, residence or pieces of furniture, that is, everything that is impermanent and shines just for one day...

Once one measures the real possibilities without having to make sacrifices, it becomes feasible to determine how far one can venture without risking subsequent grief and regret.

This correct, realistic vision of life frames it with harmony. On the other hand, unwarranted fantasy accounts for the inevitable clash with reality.

Of course, caution in decision-making must not convert into the fear of acting or the nourishment of pessimism about the future. Unbridled ambition, rashness and lack of control are what open up emotional space to the pleasure that begets pain.

Hence the social and moral vices that wither people's lives, producing the lassitude of the senses and, in the short, medium or long term, leading to madness or suicide. Some of these vices are: the *innocent cigarette* smoked in the social group as an assertion of one's personality, the elimination of a taboo, but responsible for serious respiratory problems, cancers, pulmonary emphysema; *drinking,* the cause of awful hangovers, cirrhosis of the liver, gastric and duodenal ulcers, intestinal damage and other disorders, in addition to hallucinations that lead to violence, depression, and the destruction of other people's lives and all that is dear and precious, with disastrous results; enslaving *drugs,* causing dependence with the first few uses, which seem to provide pleasure, stimulating joy, courage, self-realization, fleeting victories over powerful psychological conflicts, but turning into sometimes irreparable misfortunes...

The mistake of individuals considering themselves invincible and superior, demonstrating unawareness about the weakness and the impermanence of everything that comprises them – especially the body – fosters a deceitful pleasure, from which they awaken to profound suffering.

Nobody can escape the difficulties of life. It is programmed in such a way as to educate and strengthen, and its students cannot cheat it indefinitely.

The way to spare oneself from suffering is by confronting vicissitudes and overcoming the appeals indicative of wealth and unwarranted pleasures. And of course there are a significant number of pleasures that do not entail the risk of turning into a cause for suffering.

Suffering, therefore, when one is aware of it, is easily avoidable.

The suffering resulting from conditioning entails a flawed education and unhealthy social interaction, which produce *contaminated physical and mental aggregates.*

For many individuals, their range of values is upside down. At its base are the immediate, the risky, the vulgar and the promiscuous, in addition to temporary power and might. These are seen as what really matter in life. Consequently, their aggregates, under heavy loads of contamination, produce long-lasting physical and mental suffering.

Loud parties, young and irresponsible company, and coarse conversation may be interesting or amusing, and they may be satisfying for a while, but they are responsible for wide scale suffering.

At the same time, psychological and physical contamination derived from sickly conditionings of social groups and individuals promotes sufferings that could be avoided.

The morbid emissions of negative energy sent from one person to another ends up contaminating the latter if he or she does not have defensive, reactive means stemming from upright mental and moral conduct.

Humans live on the earth under the fear of disease, poverty, loneliness, lack of affection, failure and death. This behavior is the result of being ill-prepared for life's usual phenomena, which must be faced as part and parcel to evolution.

They are heirs to their own conscience, and also to social atavisms and unhealthy habits, among which are fears stemming from superstition, misinformation and age-old illusions, forming perturbing conditionings.

As they absorb and become imbued with these negative factors, suffering becomes unavoidable, producing psychological, mental and physical disorders through automatic somatization.

Non-threatening, ethically and morally grounded education, the kind that stimulates individuals' awareness of duty and responsibility to themselves, their neighbor and life, equips them with emotional health and spiritual courage for a balanced journey through the physical existence. This knowledge prepares them to choose what is useful and wholesome, helping them grow inwardly toward self-realization. Until this insight converts into a channeling force for their well-being, individuals will experience *suffering resulting from conditioning* stemming from their contaminated physical and mental aggregates.

3
THE ORIGINS
OF SUFFERING

According to Buddhism, the *origins of suffering* derive from internal and external conditions from which two other orders result: karma and perturbing emotions.

Of course, as the Spiritist Doctrine emphasizes, humans are the sum of their own experiences, the architects of their own destiny, which they shape by means of the impositions of determinism and free will.

This determinism – only unavoidable in some respects: birth, death, reincarnation – establishes the matrices of bodily existence, propelling individuals towards their ultimate destiny: relative perfection. The factors that program the conditions for rebirth in the physical body are the result of the acts and thoughts of previous lifetimes. Being happy as soon as possible or staying unhappy for a long time depends on one's personal free will. The choice of *how and when* to act either frees the spirit from suffering or grips it in its pincers.

Life entails the events of each moment, forming an endless chain. One action causes a corresponding reaction, generating new actions, and so on.

Thus, individuals are the result of their previous deeds. Although the effects do not always manifest immediately, this does not exempt them from having to take responsibility for their acts.

It is possible that the consequences of a failed, damaging, disastrous or harmful experience will impact others, as well as its author, after the next or next few reincarnations. The consequences, however, will arrive sooner or later. What is certain is that they will come in search of reparation.

Likewise, constructs of the good will be reflected in the individual's subsequent behavior, but might not necessarily appear right away. Since the time factor is relative, it is not all that important.

Consequently, human suffering of a karmic nature may manifest in two mutually complementing forms: trial and expiation. Both aim to educate or reeducate individuals, predisposing them to inevitable inner growth on their journey toward the plenitude awaiting them.

A trial is an experience required or proposed by the candidate's spirit guides prior to bodily rebirth, once the evolutionary records, the odds of victory and the resources within reach have been evaluated. Trials manifest as tendencies, aptitudes, limitations and possibilities under the candidate's control, as well as bearable pains and moderate joys offering the widest range of educational outcomes. Nothing is imposed; the calendar of events may be modified without any harm to the candidate's program of illumination.

Neither overly-distressing imperatives nor irreversible traumatic situations are included on the chart of commitments.

The choices about how to act multiply so that the rough edges can be smoothed out without the imposition of suffering.

Love endows individuals with excellent opportunities for changing their behavior and activities for the better, thus rendering as bearable the failure of some aspiration, the challenge of seemingly unattainable goals, or the pain of organic and mental decay, without the steep descent into the dungeons of paralysis, insanity or incurable disease.

But even if that were to happen, we could still regard it as being the candidate's personal choice, because he or she believes it to be the most effective means for future happiness, as deliverance from the harsh yoke of moral baseness.

It is possible to see evidence for such a providential choice in the candidate's resignation and courage – even joy – in the face of such painful occurrences.

Trials thus manifest rather gently: mitigating in their content and blessed in their purposes. Instead of being punitive, they educate by raising individuals' awareness, encouraging the use of the occasion in the most efficient and profitable way possible, so as to equip them to become living examples worthy of being imitated by others: apostles of love and suffering, missionaries of the good, martyrs for their ideals, even in the anonymity of their testimony.

Trials can change course and become gentler or harsher, according to how the spirit handles them.

The choice of more-difficult imperatives along the course of the evolutionary process is an act of wisdom, considering the brevity of bodily existence as opposed to the unlimited duration of the benefits obtained.

Looking at life from the causal point of view, from its origins in eternity, occurrences in the physical realm are brief, but when they end, they leave lasting marks as to how they were handled. Therefore, any struggles, sacrifices, trials and tests that recompose the soul's *tissues* – torn as a result of previous senseless attitudes – are worthwhile.

All learning requires effort in order to be assimilated, and every step upward requires persistence, strength and moral courage.

Unpleasant commitments, therefore, resurface on the landscape of reincarnation as mollifying trials that can be softened by love and mitigated by uplifting work.

Expiations, on the other hand, are different. They are irrecusably imposed as powerful medicine, as corrective surgery for a wrong that has worsened.

Similar to what happens in the criminal process, first-time offenders usually receive greater clemency resulting in a lighter sentence, and, even if their crime was very serious, they are given a certain freedom of movement without being completely restricted. Depending on the offense, repeat offenders may be fined and placed under house arrest; however, those who do not change their ways are put in prison, or if the law is barbaric, may even be submitted to the death penalty.

For comparison purposes, first-time spirit offenders are submitted to trials, whereas repeat offenders are subject to exacting expiation. Because God's love prevails in all His Laws – laws much more just than human laws – whatever the crime, they are meant to reeducate and win offenders over, rather than *eliminate* them permanently. They are never meant as revenge, but as a means of rehabilitation, for all are capable of being rehabilitated.

Imprisonment in paresis, bodily and mental limitations, paralysis, incurable congenital diseases, as well as certain types of insanity, cancers, and degenerative diseases are all expiatory resources for repeat offenders, who, in the school of trials, worsened their situation by willingly slipping into the abysses of rebellion and insanity. Amongst these offenders are premeditated suicides, cold-blooded murderers, contumacious adulterers, and blackmailers; exploiters of lives; merchants in addictive pleasures such as hallucinogenic drugs, sex, alcohol and gambling, and those who perpetrate many articles of human cruelty cataloged in the Divine Statutes.

All individuals have to live with their own conscience. In accordance with the Divine Codes deeply imprinted there, individuals collect the resonances of their respective transgressions as remedial experiences or those conducive to liberation.

In the name of love, there are cases of apparent expiations, such as individuals suffering from physical abnormalities, hearing, speech and visual impairments, paralysis, Hansen's disease and AIDS, among others, and who have chosen these conditions to teach courage and provide moral comfort to those who have grown weak in their struggles and inconsolable in their redemption.

Jesus, who never acted improperly, is the Ultimate Example.

Centuries later, Francis of Assisi, to ascend higher, chose poverty and pain, not to expiate debts but to demonstrate the greatness of the benefits.

Helen Keller, Steinmetz and many other heroes of yesterday and today have been living lessons of love in the form of selflessness, invitations to embracing happiness and the good.

Expiations may be mitigated, but not canceled.

While trials constitute a form of reparative suffering that leads to advancement, expiations only restore lost equilibrium, leading wrongdoers back to the situation they were in before their tragic failure.

On the earth, moreover, there are bearers of expiations that have no outward manifestation. These are people who agonize in cruel, internal conflicts; they are unstable and unsatisfied, unhappy and withdrawn, bearing dramas that crush and afflict them to no end. They may have a pleasant appearance and a certain appeal, but they cannot break free of their mortifying internal predicament.

The conscience is *unforgiving* when it comes to forgetting a crime. Forgiveness is only possible by means of the offender's rehabilitation.

Therefore, the origins of suffering always lie in those who bear it in the innermost part of their being, in the deep folds of their conscience.

Alongside the karmic origins of suffering, there are current causes: courting suffering through irresponsibility, hastiness and the prevalence of selfishness, which encourages individuals to make the best choice for themselves at the expense of their neighbor. This attitude manifests as perturbing emotions, which deaden the individual's aspirations and coalesce into different modalities of affliction.

Perturbing emotions spur humans today more than yesterday because of psychosocial, socioeconomic, technological, and other kinds of conflicts.

The impulses and struggles that cause people to lose their individuality, enslaving them to the standards of prevailing convention, are important triggers of suffering.

Furthermore, the loss of their sense of humor makes them sullen and artificial, generating perturbing emotions.

The lack of freedom due to constrictions of all kinds is yet another cause of suffering.

These psychological phenomena in the realm of behavior cause troubling emotions such as *desire, delusion, hatred* and *frustration.*

Because people cannot distinguish between the essential and the superfluous, what is appropriate and what is not, they extrapolate their aspirations and torment themselves with misled desire, aiming beyond what is actually possible for them and going from one disappointment to the next.

Desire is an unbridled steed that causes damage and ends up getting hurt in its mad galloping about.

The first manifestation of lucidity and balance is contentment with all that life provides. This is not a conformist attitude, with no reasonable ambition for progress, but rather a conscious acceptance of the values and resources one has received; those that promote inner harmony and well-being in relationships and in one's social group.

Excessive desire always causes suffering because it turns into a strong, *perturbing emotion,* which disrupts the delicate gears of balance.

It is said that, after a long night of revelry and debauchery, Claudius asked the infamous Messalina at dawn: "Well, are you satisfied?" To which she replied: "No; just worn out!"

A voracious fever, desire burns and annihilates one's energies. Fueled by dissatisfaction, it constantly moves from one area to another. Countless ills derive from its misguided channelization, for it is born in selfishness – that cancer of the spirit, responsible for ceaseless harm to the individual's evolution.

Even if it is meant for uplifting purposes, desire has to be managed with balance so as not to impose needs that do not correspond to reality. The ideal of the good and the effort to achieve it are expressed wholesomely and gratifyingly, becoming stimuli for the constant development of the seeds that sleep within, awaiting eclosion when the circumstances become favorable.

A consequence of *desire, delusion* – which stems from presumptuousness and pride – is a cause of suffering due to the entangling of its roots in the personality of blindly ambitious individuals, like Narcissus before his own image reflected in the pond.

The illusions of economic, social, cultural and political prosperity delude foolish individuals by leading them to believe they are superior and inaccessible to others, erecting barriers to relationships with those whom they see as having a lower *status*, as if they were a threat to their privileged position. They ignore the unavoidable biological phenomena of illness, old age and death, or they anesthetize their conscience in order not to think about the possibility of failure, a change in their status, or everyday surprises.

All these factors are causes of suffering when one intends to maintain one's prominent status, when one fears losing it, and when that actually happens.

Delusion disrupts innumerable lives that indulge in the fantasies of the physical journey, without the lucidity that discerns between the real and the spurious goals of life.

Along the same lines, the prevalence of *hatred* stands out on the landscape of human suffering. Hatred's destructive radiations consume the energies of those who feed it, and they very often strike those against whom they are directed, if they are distracted from their important duties or if they are on the same mental wavelength.

The madness of unreciprocated love, hatred uncovers the predominant presence of *aggressive instincts*, supplanting the sentiments that should govern life.

Hatred is never justified. It is responsible for the most shameful social and human calamities known to humankind.

Whenever it gains an easy foothold, it expands its roots like vigorous pincers that strangle one's reason and turn into a constant manifestation of aggression and violence.

In certain temperaments, it is like a tiny spark in a haystack, growing to produce a devouring fire. For the least important reasons, it explodes and damages everything around.

Hatred causes much suffering.

Every effort must be made to disarticulate it wherever it appears; otherwise, it spreads and causes misfortune.

Infectious and disguised as anger, anxiety, rebelliousness and other harmful reactive psychological dynamics, it contaminates with ease.

Frustration, in its turn, accounts for suffering that could be prevented if not for people's exaggerated hopes and their confused ideas of self-worth, which infuse them with false beliefs in possibilities that are not within reach.

Because people believe they are bearers of rights they do not actually possess, they become frustrated and indulge in sudden reactions of depression or anger, and they either run from life or rebelliously defy it and its values.

When individuals realize they have little or almost no personal merit, they equip themselves with harmony and faith, courage and peace in order to face challenges and overcome them, and they never let themselves be thwarted in their endeavors. If these do not provide the desired results – as is natural – they insist and persevere until they realize that their area of activity must lie elsewhere, or until they receive a favorable response to their work after all.

Love is the antidote to all causes of suffering because it proceeds from the Divine Consciousness, which generates and sustains life in all its expressions.

Enlivened by love, humans discern, aspire, act and surrender themselves with confidence, radiating life-giving energy that constantly renews them and changes the landscape around them for the better.

Love is always the wise counselor in all circumstances, efficiently guiding the individual and producing salutary results that drive progress and happiness.

At the root of any kind of suffering, the author is always the spirit itself, which, in the process of its evolution, has chosen poorly, trading the dynamics of love for those of suffering.

In order to speed recovery, the order of events is thus reversed and suffering becomes the means of leading the spirit back to love, on whose pathway plenitude is found.

Man has to cope with the problem of suffering. Eastern man wants to get rid of suffering by casting it off. Western man tries to suppress suffering with drugs. But suffering has to be overcome, and the only way to overcome it is to endure it. We learn that only from Him (Christ Crucified).

Carl Gustav Jung, *Letters*, Volume 1, Page 236.
(Princeton University Press, 1973)

4
THE END OF SUFFERING

Since suffering is a sickness, there are several effective ways to cure it. Some attenuate it; others are harmless, but very few are undisputedly effective.

A real cure, however, can only occur if the therapy uproots its causes. As long as its generating sources are not extinguished, suffering inevitably manifests.

Because the misuse of reason is what causes it, it is essential to get to the heart of its trigger so as to stop the energy that activates and vitalizes it.

In the *non-thinking* realms, where suffering results from the evolutionary phenomenon through the natural decay of forms by the disintegration of their cells and molecules, the assistance of human love attenuates its intensity, altering the circumstances and providing the lenitive of balance or health.

As thinking beings, humans are thus responsible for the preservation of other manifestations of life, and they are part of the ensemble that sustains their existence, making the evolution of all beings and vital principles possible.

Thus, attacks against and disregard for ecology are reflected in human life as much as the care for and preservation of it are. They are actions answering for their effects.

In order to end suffering, it is essential to acquire a responsible attitude capable of going back to the origins of the suffering, analyzing them and working them out with planned, purposeful direction.

Educating one's thoughts, disciplining one's habits and being sure of one's goals are skillful means for ending suffering; otherwise, therapies and techniques become mere palliatives.

In some cases, suffering is still the best therapy for human progress. While suffering, people transgress less and reflect more, resulting in reestablishing balance. A change in behavior for the worse is common once afflictive factors decrease. A thirst for wrongdoing seems to assail immature individuals, who will end up facing a future of pain-filled situations, further complicating the scant resources at their disposal. Thus, the length of time that individuals suffer contributes greatly to a correct evaluation of what they must do. Because reproachable thoughts and actions originate in personal primitivism, they induce individuals to an unhappy existence, from which they are delivered only when they resolve to climb the *mountain* of effort aimed at evolution, serenity and harmony, working the raw *metal* of the individuality and shaping it in the heat of sacrifice.

Without sacrifice, there is no moral growth or understanding of the purposes of earthly existence.

Engraved on the conscience, the Divine Laws drive the actualization of the good that lies in seed form.

If this is slow in coming, it is due to a normal maturation process that enables people to choose what they should and should not do.

The cure of an infirmity requires the extinction of its causes. Anyone that has been bitten by an adder or stung by a poisonous insect should first use a tourniquet to block the spread of the poison before combating it.

If faced with a person that has been hit by a poisoned arrow, ancient Hindu wisdom recommends pulling out the arrow first and then taking further measures.

Until the moral poisonous arrows embedded in the soul are pulled out, they will continue resisting the antidotes applied to the damage they cause, because they will keep on contaminating their victims.

Educating the mind and disciplining the will constitute the first step for rooting out the causes of afflictions, instilling fresh responsibilities, which in turn generate new, healthy outcomes to bring about the future well-being for which one is destined.

Jesus' recommendation about love is of indisputable effectiveness, in that love is the generator of values responsible for human happiness. Love mellows individuals and incites them to uplifting attitudes about life. It leads them to think before making decisions, considering which ones are most compatible with the morals and longings of the heart. Never wanting for their neighbor what they would not want to experience for themselves, they can take on commitments of prosperity without harm to themselves or others.

Lucidity generated by love leads to indiscriminate forgiveness for all people, and consequently, for oneself.

Forgetting about wrongs and abandoning plans for revenge are imperative for anyone wanting to be released from a significant amount of suffering. Depressing ideas, held on to as the result of resentment or the desire for malevolent retribution, generate infirmities that dilacerate the body's tissues and wreak havoc on the emotions. As long as they hold sway, so does suffering.

In their turn, remorse and regret for wrongful actions, in addition to the sadness and grief derived from them, are destructive mental factors that take root in the inner workings of the soul, causing long-term psychological, physical and mental disorders.

Pardoning others' wrongs brightens the inner landscape, shedding light on the shadows of the persistent anguish that blocks the joy of living, producing needless suffering.

Having had the door shut to an object of affection, or having been offended by a friend or stranger, one must always move in the direction of the other, countless open doors that await, extending fraternal understanding to wrongdoers and considering them to be unsound individuals, ignorant of the moral disease that consumes them.

Life is composed of the incessant opportunities that lie ahead, and never of the failures that occurred in the past.

Hence, like *rotten wood* cast into the *river of forgottenness*, freeing oneself of a disagreeable event is an attitude of healthy wisdom.

Such behavior makes it possible for people to be forgiven by their neighbor, who releases them from having to pay for their unfortunate moments and refrains from sending them destructive thoughts – crippling ideas – which are always assimilated by a *guilty conscience* through the phenomenon of attunement.

When one is freed from the *mental garbage* accumulated due to ignorance and futility, one's spiritual restoration begins, and a whole new activity presents itself, opening up space for health.

Included in this group of uplifting endeavors is self-forgiveness.

Considering their fragility, individuals must grant themselves the opportunity to openly right their wrongs, for the sake of their own conscience as well as for the sake of those whom they have harmed.

The ideal consciousness of self-forgiveness is not based on mechanisms of false tolerance for one's errors – that would be moral negligence, connivance and immaturity; instead, it represents a clear indication of mental and moral growth, which provides correct guidance in relation to actions for personal and general well-being.

Pure and simple repentance, if not accompanied by reparative action, is as ineffective and as harmful as the absence of it.

Moreover, a *guilt complex* is also harmful because it does not solve the wrongdoing, but makes its bad results even worse.

Self-forgiveness entails the correct mindset regarding the error and the inner satisfaction derived from the prospect of interrupting the course of the resultant damage, like pulling it up by its roots, which have become embedded in those who suffer its constriction.

It is possible to complete the endeavor of self-forgiveness by making a thorough analysis of the factors that led to the reproachable action, examining other alternatives, which were not utilized and which would not have produced adverse effects, and then being willing to adjust one's attitude, releasing oneself from the uncomfortable injunction of conflicted guilt.

If one has decided on self-renewal but finds the victim unreceptive, such should not be a reason for renewed friction, but a stimulus for pursuing one's salutary purpose, arming oneself with more patience and tolerance in order to face the reaction of the other, who, for now, is also sick but unwilling to be cured of it.

Self-forgiveness aids moral maturity because it provides a clear vision of responsibility, leading one to think carefully before taking aggressive, negligent, rash or contradictory action.

When one forgives oneself, one also learns to excuse others, offering them the same opportunity in return.

The well-being one experiences promotes the joy of offering it to the offended person, creating an aura of sympathy all around, which becomes just the right environment for release from suffering.

The actual end of suffering, therefore, occurs when, with its causes eradicated, the consequences naturally disappear.

132. What is the purpose of the incarnation of spirits?

God imposes incarnation for the purpose of leading spirits to perfection: for some, it is an expiation; for others, a mission. However, in order to reach this perfection, they must undergo all the vicissitudes of corporeal existence – therein lies their expiation. Incarnation has a further objective, which is to place spirits in situations where they can do their share in the work of creation. To this end, on each world they clothe themselves with an instrument that is in harmony with the essential matter of that world so that they may use that instrument to carry out the orders of God. In this way, they contribute to the general work and progress at the same time.

KARDEC, Allan – *The Spirits' Book*
(4th ed., ISC)

5
APPROACHES TO
END SUFFERING

Since suffering is caused by disorders in the spirit, disorders that disharmonize the flow of energy, allowing physical, mental and moral infirmities to take root, the only way to effectively end it is by getting to its cause. This will stop the disturbing wave. In a lucid mind, the result will be tranquility, which will produce health, which will radiate throughout the body, generating balance. Thus, this chain reaction will be the effectual remedy to suffering.

Until there is a real health consciousness, the individual will go from one form of suffering to another.

There are people who, although unaware of the rules promoting inner harmony, enjoy health nonetheless, appearing well-disposed and strong. These qualities, however, are automatic phenomena of the body, which may or may not be contaminated during its existence, depending on an individual's moral and mental conduct.

Ancient Buddhist wisdom established a system of meditation, through which health takes hold and suffering disappears.

Jesus, the bearer of complete balance, considered love as the sole cause for the optimal fulfillment of the individual. The subversion or absence of love for God, one's neighbor, or oneself produces dissatisfaction, maladjustment and imbalanced energies; hence, this subversion or absence is the causal factor of sickness and suffering.

Actually, the lack of love is a sickness that appears immediately or later on, marking the individual with degenerative processes in the personality that allow the body to be infected with aggressive viruses and bacilli.

The somatization of emotional problems arising from insecurity, fear, grief, hatred, rancor and jealousy is responsible for serious organic pathologies, as well as various physical ailments, producing emotional dystonias and pitiable mental disturbances.

When love – according to Jesus' concept – holds sway in individuals, it vitalizes them and radiates peace, generating a psychosphere rich in vibrations of balance, thanks to which health externalizes in a positive way, showering life with hope, altruism and uplifting accomplishments.

Spiritually sound individuals are useful and indispensable to society overall, which progresses due to their grand and dignifying contributions.

Introspection, through a profound analysis of the available resources, helps individuals find the means to put an end to suffering.

Coming from a different logical perspective, they progress toward inner harmony, sending forth a steady stream of health-preserving energy that radiates in all directions and interplays with the divine vibration: life's essential cause.

First, people must see all individuals as if they were the manifestation of their own parents, who gave them physical life – especially the mother, due to the sacrifices she willingly endured during pregnancy, childbirth and the life-preserving nourishment born in her entrails.

Even if she did not adequately fulfill her freely assumed and accepted obligations, the fact of having enabled life to manifest gives her credit as an example to be considered.

Projecting the maternal image to all living individuals – of course, without the psychoanalytic view of the torments of the libido, but with feelings of respect and tenderness – is the first step towards self-fulfillment and emotional balance, inwardly releasing any bitter or perturbing memories, which are hidden matrices for many behavioral disorders that cause suffering.

People are reborn to be free in order to grow and reach the ultimate beacon: complete self-fulfillment. Every negative emotional bond with the past becomes a constricting load that causes numerous problems.

The *image of the mother* may account for many conflicts, but it also creates healthy stimuli. Her sacrifices and dedication, her endless hours of watchfulness and her self-denial for her offspring, the songs she sang to her newborns, and all the promises that eventually came true – all deserve to be taken into account, reflected on and projected to all sentient beings.

When faced with aggression or subject to difficulties from angry, cynical, mean or abusive individuals – all unwell in any case – one should look at them as if they were one's mother during a time of weakness or fatigue, feeling unloved and alone. Instead of reacting with aggression, anger or vindictive indifference, one should use kindly patience; offer a chance for reflection, a sincere apology without resentment or acrimony. This behavior releases them from bitterness, hatred and rancor, responsible for illnesses that infiltrate easily but are difficult to eradicate.

In an extension of such affection, consideration for Mother Nature is of fundamental importance for ecological balance, and consequently for all those who contribute to its harmony.

Thus, seeing the positive, pleasant maternal aspect in all living beings provides strength for the preservation or restoration of health, release from suffering, and well-being, all which are essential conditions for happiness.

Then, after pondering and experiencing this principle, one should discover the goodness that lies dormant in all people, and which needs to be awakened and stimulated so as to bloom, flourishing and producing good fruit.

Above and beyond the dark clouds there is infinite, clear space untouched by storms.

Inside the rough, dark and shapeless diamond shines a star waiting to be brought forth by cutting and polishing.

There is no one who does not possess inner goodness. In the folds of the soul lies God's presence, like coagulated light, awaiting outside stimuli in order to shine with maximum power.

Aggressive people, who delight in tormenting others, thereby producing suffering, are bearers of much inner pain, which they try to hide under the mask of violence, false superiority and delusion.

Even wild animals become friendly when domesticated, and in receiving vibrations of love, they alter the constitution of their aggressive instinct, changing their behavior, attesting to the presence of the Divine Consciousness in seed form in everything and everyone.

It is an acquisition of wisdom to be able to reach into people's latent goodness, seeking to tune in to that frequency of life, rather than being bound only to their outward manifestations, their defensive-aggressive reactions, which carry morbific vibrations that unleash many of the ills responsible for suffering.

From the experience of identifying the goodness in people in general comes the extraordinary achievement of discovering God's Presence everywhere, in all creatures, establishing emotional bonds for conscious interaction, since, unconsciously, individuals are inescapably interdependent. Enabling the automatic phenomenon of interaction to become lucid is a valid endeavor that fosters human progress, entailing the development of more eloquent and significant skills.

Life is a constant challenge, rich with opportunities for growth and immersion in its deepest mysteries, which increasingly prove to be ever more magnificent and fascinating. Hence, the development of the spirit's intellectual and moral values never stops.

Pain and suffering are generally more primitive stages of the development process, which, through afflictive sensations and emotions, propel individuals toward higher planes, where the stimuli are different and much more inviting. Since God's Presence lies in everything and everyone, it is necessary to discover in them the goodness that expresses their divine essence and origin.

At that stage, the desire to repay this goodness, this divine presence, must be emphasized.

Universal harmony results from a diversity of forms, expressions and presentations in subtle processes of syntony, of similarity.

Likewise, when any important quality is identified, especially the goodness in people, animals, and in the lofty purposes of plant life, one should plan to repay that sentiment.

From the starting point of intention, and as a natural means of repayment, one should let the desire to give back increase the goodness that is already more developed in one's inner world.

Step by step, from thought to words to action, intent grows and becomes a creative, reciprocating reality developing important resources all around. This movement of positive energy represents a healthy effort to prevent suffering or be released from it.

Goodness is a small effort that comes from the duty to joyfully repay all the gifts that people enjoy without realizing it or putting forth any effort, automatically, like the sun, the moon and the stars, the sky, air, landscapes, water, plants and animals, and which humans inadvertently have been consuming, polluting unconscionably and killing mercilessly...

Life makes aggressors against nature pay for their negative interference in its order and structure.

Thus, reciprocating nature's goodness is to respect its codes of existence, of survival, fostering its increase, continuity and life per se, wherever it is expressed. This goodness, which can be seen as a retributive duty, makes room for other ways to manifest it.

Noble sentiments that have not been stimulated to action for a long time become blunted, weakened, and nearly disappear. Hence, goodness grows through practice, becoming a habit or disappearing for lack of use.

Choosing to act or not to act with goodness is a decision of the mind, and producing the good is of the *heart*.

There is in all beings the *instinct to preserve life* and a natural inclination to the good, since they are *God's heirs* learning how to use the resources at their disposal.

The choice of pathway depends on whether one is interested in immediate results, or whether one prefers long-lasting fruits later by giving up the immediate ones.

The long and sometimes difficult ascent will ultimately be successful by virtue of the destiny assigned to all beings. Making it bright and pleasant should be the choice of all who yearn to end their suffering.

The practice of goodness makes possible the prevalence of love, whose full attainment crowns life, freeing it from all its shackles. Love is the vibration of the Father expanding towards His children and flowing out from them in all directions. Even the cruelest individuals, the most insensitive tormenters, experience flashes of love in waves of tenderness, caring gestures, expressions of sacrifice...

Instinctively, animals risk their lives to preserve the lives of their offspring, revealing the immanent presence of love in non-thinking form.

In humans, love blazes and creates heroism, the self-sacrifice with which life towers above and triumphs over death, like perennial day over transient night.

Expanding the immanent sentiment that harmonizes with the *soul of life* pulsating in everything, the practice of love fosters the end of suffering, should it exist. Love is the most powerful antidote for any degenerative phenomena that take the form of pain, ingratitude, aggression, imbalance, crime or disgrace. It has ingredients that dilute evil and favor the emergence of the hidden good.

Wherever progress thrives, love manifests. There are exceptions, as in the case of horizontal growth, in which self-interest and greed foster economic, technological and social development... But even then, love is present, although directed toward selfishness and the satisfaction of the senses, from which it will then give rise to altruistic gestures that provide joy to others, and widespread well-being...

Without taking the first step, nobody can go the distance.

Selfishness is the sometimes pernicious ground zero for the first steps toward solidarity and the common good. Worse than selfishness is disinterest, the morbidity of indifference, implying that love is dead, albeit only dormant, waiting for the right stimulus to awaken.

Life is impossible without love.

In the same way that crime is disguised and the lower sentiments are veiled behind various masks, there are a number of positive ways in which people reflect the love that they have not yet realized. As love grows, it neutralizes suffering, and its presence contributes to ending the degenerative causes of suffering. When love reaches a high degree in just one person, it annuls rage and hatred along with their countless victims, as well as their promoters.

Radiating outward like the light, love dominates every nook and cranny and draws everything toward its generating center of energy.

Love is synonymous with moral health, and those who possess it eliminate the poisonous causes that propagate, producing suffering.

Love is subtle, sensitive, patient and constant; it is never annoying or imposing. However, those who experience it never forget it. Even if its flow is momentarily interrupted, it always resumes.

At the root of every noble action is the sap of love, producing and sustaining life.

Using this life-giving energy is a duty, and with lucid awareness of its magnitude, applying it for the sake of harmony puts an end to suffering. Love is a positive vibration that engenders enthusiasm and optimism, giving color to one's existence. It restores the tired soil of the heart and drains the swamp in which the pestilence of the passions has let hope and joy decompose.

Nobody loves inertly.

Love is dynamic; it leads to constructive activity, responsible for progress.

Always seeking the good, love focuses its forces on it and never gives up before reaching the goal, and even then, it remains supportive so as to keep the individual from languishing away and plunging into dismay.

Since suffering arises from dissatisfaction, dystonia, the degeneration of the tissues and maladjusted biological phenomena, love acts on the molecules as a vitalizing wave, and as it restores their balance, it overcomes suffering, interrupting its causal flow.

However, when physical pain persists as a result of organic disorders, resignation and the courage of love dampen its effects, making them bearable and producing heroes of suffering, whose agony of whatever kind makes them models that give strength and dignity to others, thus embellishing moral and human life on earth.

Under the power of love, new, positive karmic dynamics are set in motion, interrupting those of a pernicious nature, for good negates evil and its consequences, freeing transgressors of the laws once they begin to abide by them and right their wrongs.

Love is what leads to fraternal piety and compassion, inducing individuals to solidarity and even sacrifice.

There is a kind of compassion, which, not resulting from the dynamic action of profound love, may be harmful and even depressing. It is the kind that bemoans suffering and discourages those who experience it, as a way of haloing them with misery, abandonment, bad luck and misfortune. This attitude results from a mistaken view of suffering that imparts the perspective that suffering is an arbitrary punishment and a perturbing injustice.

Compassion joins fellowship, which shares the sentiments of others without weakening their moral resistance. It encourages them to persevere in their ideals and cherished principles, which drive them to continue advancing without the possibility of regressing.

Compassion for the good – the fruit of love – leads individuals to act appropriately, changing the shape of suffering with the chisel of tenderness that smooths off the rough edges. This sentiment is similar to the soft moonlight on a dark night, spreading its tenuous and comforting glow over the landscape. It promotes a propitious vision of useful activities where the shadows of discouragement, fear and growing despair once predominated.

Passion for the spiritual endeavor radiates constructive compassion, which encourages benevolence and philanthropy, endowing compassion with fraternal vigor, thanks to which the sentiments of solidarity express love in its many facets.

The lack of compassion degrades individuals, and the lack of passion for the good makes them rebellious – if not morbidly indifferent, like mummified observers of the everyday events of life.

Doing work for the good, with the corresponding passion to keep at it, becomes fulfilling charity for both giver and receiver. It gives rise to a two-fold action: the receiver's satisfaction and the giver's inner response in the form of a tranquil conscience due to the emotion experienced.

Life always responds according to the way it is questioned. Every action results in an equivalent reaction, triggering subsequent effects that in turn generate new results.

In order to interrupt this cycle when pernicious, compassion for oneself and others is necessary, for it leads to constructive actions where dynamics triggering results favorable to progress can take hold, thus interrupting the wave that causes suffering.

Christ's love for all is a constant stimulus for people to have compassion on one another, upholding one another in suffering and difficulties, never worsening one another's needs or afflicting one another through the *aggressive instincts* that could still prevail in their *animal nature*.

Compassion is vitally important in human behavior. It leads to the realization of the fragility of bodily existence and all the enticements that disguise it.

Whereas illusion is responsible for ceaseless suffering, compassion exposes it.

Since individuals render earthly life a fantasy with their chimeras and dreams, reality undoes this childish image, causing suffering for all those who, in their immaturity, put too much trust in the transience of forms and physical appearance, promises of eternal love and fidelity, joy without sorrow, and noon without twilight at the end of the journey.

Thus, the death of illusion wounds those who entrusted their physical existence to it, without reservation, without caution.

Illusion is therefore an anesthetic for the spirit.

Of course, a bit of fantasy frames life and gives it stimulus. However, to establish oneself and construct one's future on illusion's fragile foundations is like trying to build on quicksand or marshy soil covered by still water only on the surface.

There are those who postpone reality, avoiding it in order not to suffer... And there are those who try to establish themselves on harsh realism, which is often nothing but another erroneous form of illusion.

Awareness of reality results from observing daily events, the transience of the so-called objective world, and a peaceful, lucid analysis about what is true in relation to what is apparent, what is essential in relation to what is secondary, and so on.

Self-compassion – self-love – enables one to have a realistic, non-aggressive vision of the purposes of earthly existence, stimulating one's compassion for one's neighbor – love for others – understanding their struggle and offering them a hand in order to uphold them or help them up so they may continue on their journey.

Instead of producing a pessimistic, bitter and skeptical outlook as the result of the death of illusion, such an attitude encourages and enhances, giving meaning and significance to all events.

Therefore, compassion becomes an element that puts a halt to suffering, as a natural result of the other steps, moving from emotion to action.

Thus, in the area of behavior, the need arises to act virtuously, selflessly, transforming one's purposes into ennobling accomplishments.

All human experiences are tools that enable individuals to mature. Some derive from immediate duties and are common to everyone, a natural phenomenon, without which they would experience inevitable alienation with all its pernicious consequences.

The fact that people participate in the social context, even if they do so without unusual or extraordinary deeds, equips them with emotional resources that shape their existence, beautifying it with increasing stimuli for its continuation.

With regard to the means for putting an end to suffering, we have already explained that meritorious actions are preponderant, especially those that are unusual, that portray noble temperaments and selfless sentiments.

Pursuing unusual, unfamiliar activities is a means of seeking enlightenment through the realization of all that converges inwardly to that end.

Those who accumulate wealth intend to use it for specific purposes. Those who have wisdom think about increasing it at the time they apply it, selecting the most profitable ventures, either from an economic or an emotional standpoint. This attitude promotes progress, generates opportunities for service, and dignifies lives that were once under the threat of despair and worthlessness.

Likewise, spiritual and emotionally lofty resources should be channeled to uncommon, high-minded activities that many dare not undertake.

Uncommon actions range from invaluable material contributions made with love and tenderness, to the extraordinary gesture of remaining silent when offended, forgiving when assailed, and forgetting when harmed.

All those who use the solvent of love to dissolve the negative forces that insist on obstructing their progress avoid contamination, and if already affected, they bounce back, ending the causes and thus the suffering.

A defenseless mental field enables the barbs of evil to proliferate, infesting it with pestiferous residues responsible for countless ailments.

Defense against harmful factors is only possible when the emission of healthy energy vitalizes the psyche, which reflects the aspirations of the spirit, protecting the spirit against outside aggressions. By not generating destructive thoughts or accumulating the disruptive vibrations of hate, fear, jealousy, resentment, grief, or lust, one does not become victim to degenerative internal content.

This inner state stimulates high-minded, uncommon acts, which is the next step to enlightenment.

Only by becoming enlightened can individuals overcome all suffering; eradicating its causes, they safeguard themselves against destructive attacks.

Enlightenment results from the inner search for the Self, a wise choice in relation to the *ego* that prevails in the mapping of the more immediate human aspirations, those agents of vital disruptions and overwhelming failures in the struggle, which the brief corporeal existence is.

The development of the *divine spark* innate in all individuals deserves every sacrifice and undertaking in order to burn in its full splendor, overcoming the stubborn shadows that are the lengthy heritage of lifetimes on the primitive levels of the initial process of evolution.

True enlightenment advances individuals who, surpassing the limiting contingencies of the carnal phase, annul all causes of suffering, effectively putting an end to them. They no longer need pain to reach their goals, because love is their sole reason for living, in tune with the Divine Thought that attracts them more and more vigorously toward the ultimate goal.

6
ALTRUISM

Altruism is a living lesson in charity, a higher expression of ennobled love that opens the door to action, without which it would be pointless.

An expansion of solidarity, altruism attains its most significant expression when it distributes blessings and shares afflictions, working to minimize the latters' effects by eradicating their causes.

Altruism is the very love taught by Jesus Himself, the kind that practices selflessness to focus on the welfare of others, forgetting all wrongs in order to expand by means of aspirations related to progress, order and happiness.

The antithesis of selfishness, it heals the wounds of the soul caused by it and fosters comprehensive health.

Altruism is a bright and shining star radiating an enveloping peace that reaches and overcomes the emotional and prejudicial distances that keep people apart. It captures all willing hearts with its radiation, and indelibly marks the periods of life with its presence.

The desire for possession, gratification of the senses and superiority, which typifies selfishness, becomes a yearning for selflessness, happiness and fraternity in the liberating arena of altruism.

The very nature of desire changes. It loses the tormenting aspect of being a game of pleasures and becomes an aspiration for service.

The impulses of the flesh, which seek to satisfy the instincts and the strongest, most primordial passions, become delights of human kindness and understanding.

One's neighbors are no longer objects to be used but to be honored. All stimuli are directed toward helping them grow and triumph over false needs, developing their awakening virtues so that their spiritual nature may overcome the dominant, animal nature.

The existence of altruism is revealed by various sentiments of moral greatness, which give dignity to life. Generosity assumes a prominent role among these sentiments because it is altruism's primary practical manifestation, and thus its initial form externalized in action.

It is customary to say that those who do not open their hand keep their heart closed. This is true, for generosity begins as a materialized sentiment that loves and desires to be of assistance.

Opening one's hand is the gesture of letting the generous flow of giving pour forth from the heart to the outside world in order to manifest the grand forms of self-denial in the future. Therefore, generosity gives things, objects, utensils, food, clothing, shelter, etc. at first, and then offers sentiments, honing the art of serving to the point of selfless dedication.

Only those who practice giving material things become predisposed to offering transcendent gifts, those that are priceless, those that "do not corrode," or "thieves steal."

Generosity is enriched the more it is distributed, and is multiplied the more it is divided, for all that one offers, one possesses, but whatever one holds on to becomes a debt. Hence, happiness is the result of the act of giving and the benefits derived from it.

Generous individuals radiate friendliness and generate a sense of well-being wherever they are.

The visceral enemy of selfishness, generosity pulls out by the roots the pincers of selfishness, the cause of suffering.

When Jesus was on the cross, suffering from human ingratitude, He even assisted the thief who pleaded for His help, generously promising him the *Kingdom of Heaven,* which began to take hold in the thief's mind and heart from that moment on.

As altruism expands, it takes on an ethical aspect.

We can see this ethic as being the serenity that respects all behaviors without imposing its own way of living, of looking at life, of expressing itself. Besides being a moral ethic, it has a universal character, overcoming interests and geographical conventions, which establish concepts of convenience based on prejudices and limitations, and on transitory laws that may be necessary at times but not intended for the common good.

Thus, there are ethics that support slave states, restrict freedom of movement, hinder procreation, persecute those who disagree with their codes, and punish and destroy at will.

The ethics of generosity focuses its attention on *Natural Law* or the *Law of Love,* which respects life at every stage and protects all sentient beings, promoting their expansion.

The Spirit benefactors of humanity gave Allan Kardec complete ethical guidelines derived from Natural Law and therefore from God, to be expressed in other laws, which foster progress, preserve life and dignify all. These laws use labor to advance humans, all of whom are equal in origin, yet different in intellectual and moral achievements that are without privilege but within the reach of all.

This ethic enables people to tell right from wrong and drives them to acquire a higher consciousness, the result of choosing positive values, which make life worth living.

Its morality is centered on benevolence, without the mistake of consenting to error or any attack against the codes of order, duty and justice.

Its entire framework of responsibility aims to promote individuals and their *habitat,* since they are all dependent on one another.

It does do not choose certain individuals over others, although its expression of love varies according to the affective responses. But this does not invalidate the need to overcome the obstinacy of wrongdoers and see them too as being in need of benevolence, which can and should be offered to them.

Normally, under the action of desire, other people are classified according to the interest they elicit and the profit they can generate, rendering them affable and friendly, unfriendly or hostile, indifferent or insignificant. Later on, the sentiments of possessive love, disaffection and hatred, and those of disinterest or indifference manifest. The ethic of benevolence proposes the developing of hidden values in some, and understanding in those who judge others who do not match the model to which they have been submitted.

The ethic of benevolence is not repressive since it is devoid of a punitive nature; nevertheless, its critical thinking analyzes everything and everyone in order to produce the best.

The ethic of benevolence is peaceful. As such, it may be regarded as the acquisition of serenity, according to its deep meaning in Sanskrit.

Consequently, it is patient; it does not rush into things, nor does it seek immediate results.

Patience is the next step in implementing altruistic intent.

There is an interrelationship between the various requirements for the full experience of altruism, which eradicates the causes of suffering. One factor depends on the other, and all are achievements of the spirit in its quest for perfection.

Each factor becomes a healthy exercise in moral elevation and promotes the sentiments, developing the intellect in the art of understanding in order to serve, of growing in order to become free, of acquiring knowledge in order to distribute it.

To this avail, patience is highly important; it creates conditions for each accomplishment at the proper time: neither postponement, hastiness nor impulsiveness, for they do not lead to the hoped-for results.

Patience harmonizes human aspirations, teaching the value of well-prepared, continuous action, which attends to each task in a timely manner.

Patience enables one to redo any failed work with the same enthusiasm, and it teaches one how to go about it most efficiently, without the fatigue that leads to pessimism and giving up. It knows that what cannot be done today can be done later, if one perseveres.

Life keeps on growing, molecule by molecule, in an atmosphere of harmony, patience and relentless activity.

Patience stimulates courage, which strives to bring the results in line. This courage is the result of knowing the laws that provide persistence in the program of altruism.

Courage is a moral quality for facing the struggle and persevering in it, never giving up on it for any reason. Ongoing effort allows for the continuation of the action, which accomplishes the set program.

The eradication of the causes of suffering is only possible through the effort one commits to that task; without such effort it fails, delaying the eradication.

Well-directed effort characterizes the degree of an individual's evolution. More prevalent in some than others, it sets them apart, attesting to their achievements while enabling them to see how much is yet to be done.

Thus, seriously persisting to acquire altruism by engaging in activities that must be completed step by step is a sure means of freeing oneself from suffering.

Hence, people's character is measured by their efforts to grow and improve in order to face the reactions that their ideals and undertakings cause.

Those who yield to obstacles, who give up in the face of difficulty, have already lost the battle without having engaged it. Often, obstacles and difficulties are more apparent than real, more threatening than actually impeditive. One can only evaluate them after having confronted them. In addition, each victory becomes a refinement in the way of accomplishing something, and each defeat a lesson on what not to do. This achievement is the result of committed persistence without discouragement after each small or big failure. The goal must be reached; therefore, the courage of continued effort is indispensable.

It is often necessary to stop to reflect, to retreat in order to renew one's strength to continue to move forward. A sound strategy involves giving up what is of minor importance now in order to gain lasting, significant results later.

Effort encourages the development of dormant inner resources. People grow as they accomplish something. The proper channeling of their efforts has a boosting effect, for the pull toward degrading practices, which break down one's moral resistance, is also a compelling force, which should be aimed at higher realizations.

Altruism cannot manifest without effort, since there seems to be a conspiracy on the part of selfishness to prevent it from taking hold of the emotions.

The computer can store millions and millions of bytes of data, and like any other device that fascinates people, it resulted from the efforts of those who engineered it and input the information, bit by bit.

Life perishes without effort. Unused limbs lose their flexibility, wither and die.

Another essential key to altruism is focus on it; otherwise the mind strays, opening cracks for pessimistic, discouraging ideas to enter.

Focusing the mind on an altruistic action allows for the establishing of an effective plan for deciding on techniques and gathering resources to carry it out.

Focus expands individuals' horizons while strengthening them inwardly by providing for the exchange of higher energies that vitalize them, renewing their energies when depleted, especially during an altruistic endeavor.

Unaccustomed to lofty gestures, people react against them. They become aggressive and ungrateful, and acknowledge the positive results only later. This attitude quite often discourages selfless, unprepared individuals, who retreat or give up because they did not seek the support of meditation first, and consequently let themselves be poisoned by such toxicity.

As one ponder the matter, one can see the need for greater, sacrificial, altruistic contributions; one will understand that the immense lack of love is responsible for so much hardheartedness, and that widespread aggression attests to the severity of people's increasing moral sickness.

Meditation expands one's vision concerning evil. At the same time, it equips one with lucidity, providing the right tools for dealing with this cruel adversary.

The art of concentration is a valuable and time-consuming acquisition that needs to be cultivated and practiced in order to respond effectively to people's emotional needs.

People are used to focusing on phenomena resulting from the passions or stronger sensations, such as desire, jealousy, hatred, resentment, sensuality, gluttony and vices in general, so when it comes to higher and more refined aspirations, they make excuses, stating that they cannot focus, that they lack the ability to stick to the subject out of mental habit, or due to lack of courage to face the responsibilities that come with a change of routine.

Without focus, all activities lose their meaning and are poorly executed. Focus heightens the details, the particular and overall vision of the undertaking, reinvigorating individuals and providing clarity and inspiration.

All the great achievers owe their success to focus, effort and patience. They ignored everything else when focused on a goal.

Of course, their tenacity was the result of longstanding experience, providing them with the growing ability to mentally block out all other interests and focus solely on the task at hand.

Focus illuminates and invigorates altruism in difficult times by enabling one to understand the circumstances surrounding the events and problems in which people become entangled. Focus also endows it with special energy that radiates outward in waves of well-being that permeate all who approach the one who exerts it. And the more one practices it, the greater one's ability to exteriorize its energy. Hence, focus is essential to altruism because it annuls the causes of suffering by bringing to the forefront the higher sentiments of life in full realization of the good.

Finally, after living according to the above items, wisdom takes hold in people's minds and hearts. Wisdom frees them from ignorance, points out the real purpose of physical existence, and stimulates them to pursue increasingly alluring and pleasing new endeavors beckoning ahead.

Wisdom is often confused with intellectual knowledge, a sophisticated mind and the acquisition of culture, which, although valuable, are horizontal achievements.

And it is essential that, alongside this important acquisition, the enlightened and profound sentiment of love becomes the great vertical of the evolutionary process.

This vertical achievement is responsible for the discernment of how to act, providing logical resources for such, while at the same time softening with affection the occasional roughness of the implementation process.

Wisdom renders love prudent. It makes it a benevolent, giving, altruistic sentiment and keeps it from degrading into sentimentality, which hides the schemes of the sickly *ego*. At the same time, wisdom provides the intellect the peaceable perception that reason must join forces with the humane, serene and kindly sentiment because that is what persuades people.

Wise persons recognize the vast area lying before them to be conquered and thus they live more than they speak, and teach more by example than by words.

When the steps conducive to altruism are developed and wisdom is acquired, the spirit is enlightened and life makes sense. The limits of time and space are surpassed in light of the grand goal to be reached.

Suffering then gives way to peace because its karmic causes disappear, overcome by new, liberating actions. And since negative causes are no longer generated in the present, the future is not bleak or threatening. Thus, altruism thrives in the mind and heart, and it is no longer the man or the woman that lives, but Christ that lives in them, as Paul stressed and other martyrs experienced, along with the heroes and sages of all times, who embraced altruism for humanity's sake.

7

CAUSES OF SUFFERING

In the relentless pursuit of pleasure, people go from one sensation to the next, without realizing that this instability causes the anxiety responsible for the overwhelming suffering that threatens to plunge them into despair. Until they decide to choose legitimate values over those they deem meaningful, but which are mere *illusions,* they will find it very hard to commit to a path that will bring about peace.

Living under the demands of a machine that imposes real needs and predisposes them to imaginary and disturbing ones, people opt for the latter. These entail the sensations of the domineering *ego,* pressuring them to pursue the coarsest aspirations at the expense of the subtle, ennobling ones that thrive in selflessness, high-minded effort, self-denial, and the cultivation of the inner life in the realm of the spirit over matter.

The body should be regarded as a transitory instrument for the eternal being, a temporary sanctuary for the higher purpose of enabling the soul to evolve by means of the enlightening experiences it affords it in the moral, spiritual and intellectual arenas, as well as by the practice of virtue. It should never be an instrument used to cater to the sensations that characterize its molecular constitution.

Of course, this does not entail ascetic, isolationist behavior, which fosters the escape from apparent reality. What matters is for the mental life to shape the physical. One can change places without changing one's conduct, living outwardly in one place and inwardly in the other. The lack of attunement between these two ways of living causes individuals to break down due to the appearance of neuroses and devastating psychoses, imposing suffering that could be avoided if they could only get a better grasp of life's goals.

A rational and lucid examination of one's real needs provides healthy guidance that offers the reward of inner harmony and emotional balance.

The inordinate pursuit of things, entertainment and enjoyment can never fill the pleasure void; on the contrary, it frustrates those who fall into its traps.

There are individuals who have considerable wealth, social prestige, fame and intelligence, thanks to which they can acquire whatever they please, travel wherever they want, and relate with all sorts of different people, and yet they are tormented by *emptiness,* boredom and dissatisfaction – powerful causes of suffering.

They invariably place events and interests outside their reality, in the outer world, and consider them a source of suffering or enjoyment, depending on whether they can benefit from them or not. However, the issue is more profound and important for their inner life. In the absence of real, inner meaning, their apparent one is lost the moment it is attained. Herein lies the largest number of frustrations and dissatisfactions that cause suffering.

Something has worth only when it inspires the same meaning for all people, who project their inner needs and true aspirations toward achieving it.

The beautiful places and rich, cosmopolitan cities that impress some individuals, causing a strong desire to live there, awaken unease, discomfort and displeasure in others. Island paradises and spiritual retreats enthrall some, but cause conflicting feelings, anguish and unbearable despair in others. Haute couture and fine jewelry intensify greed in some, but have no effect on others who show no interest in them and do not suffer at all if they do not possess them.

The search for reality, the Self, must begin with a deep, inward analysis of life's real needs, and never with the preference for adornments, objects and situations. These only emphasize the *ego* and perturb it, making it proud and boastful, or, in their absence, bitter, resentful, fearful...

First, one must acquire a state of spiritual peace to experience everything without becoming attached to anything.

The flame that shines outwardly projects a light but casts a shadow, whereas the light that shines inwardly radiates equally in all directions without producing any shadows.

The mind and the body susceptible to pain due to the possession or loss of outer things will always experience long periods of suffering, going from one form to another without breaking free from it. Liberation will occur only when people empty themselves of ambition, embracing inner selflessness and overcoming desire.

The act of wanting (desiring for oneself, expressing attachment) is the foreshadowing cause of loss (transfer to another, because what is held on to is owed, not possessed), thus evoking ownership, responsible for anxiety, insecurity and fear – all generators of suffering.

Self-knowledge helps one understand what is useful or superfluous, essential or secondary for a happy life.

Expendable acquisitions weigh on one's emotional economy and become a concern that diverts the mind from the goals it should pursue.

Jesus wisely said that the Son of Man does not have a stone on which to lay His head, although the birds in the sky, the snakes and beasts all have nests and dens,[4] demonstrating His total detachment from all the things that overwhelm people with tension and restlessness.

To the young man who wanted to follow Him, He explained that one thing was still missing: "Sell everything and give the money to the poor." The young man, who claimed to be just and Law-abiding, was nonetheless enveloped by and lost in the trifles of the world to which he was attached... And he did not follow Him.

It is very difficult to break free from atavisms – those belongings and habits that pervade one's behavior – to begin constructing a new, prevailing nature. Under the burden of such dependencies, individuals fail to see the light, to discern the goal, to free themselves in order to find themselves.

They confuse peace with the tranquility backed by their possessions, which give them comfort and social prominence, but also arouse envy. Moreover, possessions may be lost at any moment due to the normal vicissitudes that catch everyone off guard – death, for instance, which forces them to leave everything behind, but does not always bring release, for torments continue beyond the physical dimension...

---

[4] Allusion to Luke 9:58 and Matt. 8:20 – Tr.

Suffering must be overcome by love, meditation and the understanding of its presence in the lives of all beings as a cause of progress, a need for reeducation and a mechanism of evolution that lingers in discerning individuals who think for themselves, since the goal of reincarnation is to triumph over it.

8
PATHWAYS TO HEALTH

D ue to the individual's incomplete moral development, suffering is the road to spiritual redemption. A personal choice, it is a road devoid of punitive action; rather, it educates or reeducates using the same mechanisms through which the individual incurred a moral debt, strayed off course, or disregarded the Laws of Life in the first place. Suffering prevails as long as purification is necessary. The only exceptions entail collective enlightenment, that is, when the missionaries of love and the good plunge into the world's darkness in order to illuminate it with their examples. Since they no longer need moral and physical pain, they choose or accept it as a willing hardship in order to teach courage, selflessness and sacrifice to those in the rearguard engaged in ignorance, illusion, rebellion, violence, selfishness and denial of duty – all being causes of suffering, sickness and pain.

Complete health, peace and inner joy result from mental clarity, which chooses appropriate acts for a life of spiritual growth.

As long as people are not persuaded to seek balance, that is, the optimal homeostasis between the psyche and the physical body, they will remain entangled in all kinds of suffering. Suffering is a warning indicating a deviation from the path of harmony, and appears in the form of compromised, blocked or unbalanced energy, promoting the onset of all kinds of diseases, misfortunes and woes.

Of course, conventional therapies do help with the recovery of health and its relative maintenance. However, only the internal factors that account for emotional and social behavior can create the conditions that support a permanent state of well-being, eradicating causes of pain or providing new, compensatory ones if the former have not yet been eradicated, thus promoting structural balance.

Jesus summed up love as a powerful force for annulling the unfortunate causes of suffering and obtaining compensation through practicing the good.

In compliance with the lessons of the Gospel and the guidelines proposed by the high order Spirits, Allan Kardec, alluding to Jesus, presented charity as the true road to salvation, the acquisition of complete health.

For charity – love in its highest expression – to be authentic, it requires the illumination of those who practice it, affording them, at the same time, a constant refinement of purposes that lead to self-denial and victory over the primitive, dominant tendencies.

Due to its extraordinary emotional content, charity mellows the benefactor and blesses the beneficiary, dignifying, advancing and helping the latter surmount him or herself. That is why it truly is a profound action that requires special requisites acquired through the constant effort of spiritual growth.

Centuries ago, Buddha recommended an *eight-fold path for salvation*. These eight steps are indispensable for enlightenment through love and plenitude through happiness.

Human beings always believe, even in that which they deny. Their very act of denying is a form of believing, which they defend with enthusiasm and vigor. Denial, therefore, is a type of affirmation that demonstrates a natural or rational belief concerning their conviction.

Believing rightly, however, means directing the thought in a positive, uplifting way, anchoring it in sound purposes conducive to the successful achievement of the principles one believes in.

This is a stimulating belief that lends beauty to life's mechanisms and sets them in motion, deeply altering one's behavior for the better and proposing a life based on the power of faith.

In dealing with all the sick who came to Him, Jesus was peremptory in requiring that they believe both in Him and in the recovery of their health.

His affirmative response would create an organic reaction favorable for the movement of the energy blocked by sickly conditionings, by karmic consequences responsible for degenerative disorders in the body, mind or emotions. The ailing person's mental and emotional opening up to the certainty that recovery was indeed possible and that Jesus could bestow it provided the receptivity needed for an immediate cure.

Thus, *faith can do all* because it triggers one's unexplored inner mechanisms that bring forth untapped forces, completely changing the internal and, subsequently, the external landscape.

"Faith moves mountains," Jesus stated. Faith is the channel for every mental possibility because it changes the action of habitual forces. When faith is present, it fosters action and vibrates inwardly, generating energies that vitalize the entire machinery through which it moves.

Believing rightly provides an optimistic view of life that becomes enriched with motivations that nothing can perturb. Believing rightly also knows how to wait, and it encourages the continued pursuit of the endeavor, even when the circumstances seem to conspire against it, causing confusion.

All of humankind's achievements began with the act of believing rightly, which motivated people to persist in turning their mental plans into objective reality.

Nicolaus Copernicus, believing rightly in the heliocentric system, suffered constant humiliation and struggled against sectarianism, intolerance, fanaticism and ignorance, until he was proven right.

Christopher Columbus, intuitively *remembered* lands unknown to European civilization, and believing rightly, in spite of being discouraged and mocked by his contemporaries and the Courts, to which he turned for help, he discovered America, proving that he was right.

Believing rightly leads to *wanting rightly*.

One of the causes of human suffering is wanting wrongly, true to the illusion of immediate and delusional pleasure, which chooses the expendable in detriment of the essential, the temporary rather than the permanent. And to get it, people act out their negative tendencies, compromising themselves morally and spiritually.

This wanting wrongly enslaves people to the lower passions, whose shackles inexorably keep them bound to the unfortunate effects of their choice.

For their own enjoyment, people want what is not appropriate. They let selfishness override the common good, and they harm all those who try to stop them or get in their way.

Wanting rightly proposes methods compatible with the goals of one's belief. Incorrect means are not justifiable for noble purposes because they denigrate ideals, which must remain pure. Without the use of corresponding means, achievements lose their otherwise praiseworthy quality.

The much-coveted so-called conveniences that people long for are actually a way of avoiding the appropriate, sometimes complex channels that comprise the framework of wanting rightly.

This does not mean that easier accomplishments signify a deviation from the goal. There are many of them, as is natural. However, they should not become the general rule, discouraging other accomplishments requiring greater effort, persistence and sacrifice.

Those who aim for the mountaintop cannot avoid the difficult ascent, for it is part and parcel to their intention.

The act of wanting renders challenges and difficulties less harsh.

Wanting to spread Jesus' message rightly, Paul used the most strenuous efforts, suffering illnesses, abandonment, stoning and almost death, stating confidently: "Woe is unto me if I do not preach the Gospel." Living his ideal took sacrifice.

Committing oneself to wanting rightly rejects ignoble proposals, even when they appear to be a "silver bullet."

Anything that does not bear the seal of correctness belittles the quality of the action.

Jesus always wanted rightly and hence always acted rightly, making His message an indelible light shining throughout the centuries, overcoming disfigurements, interpolations and regrettable adulterations.

When one believes and truly wants to believe rightly, one *uses words* that reflect that fact, and, according to the Gospel, such words manifest what the *heart is filled with.*

Therefore, living the higher aspirations inwardly is essential so that the symphony of one's words may rightly convey them outwardly.

Words are a valuable communication tool that has paralyzed many great ideals of humanity for not being true to the sentiments that should be expressed.

People talk for the sake of talking; they talk in order to conceal emotions and ideals; they talk with sordid or harmful purposes in mind.

The word that liberates can also enslave.

Therefore, the art of talking entails requisites that are essential for expressing oneself rightly.

Talking should be discerning, knowing how and when to say something, and it should avoid causing embarrassment and resentment.

There is no scarcity of accusers and pointless, shallow, ironic and ambiguous talkers in the world. Dominated by false idealisms and inferior passions, they disturb and criticize, causing unhappiness and trouble.

Talking rightly fosters progress, developing aspirations that manifest in the ideals of freedom and love, stimulating individuals to pursue the good.

By talking rightly, Socrates developed philosophy, elevating it to the heights and promoting the ethical and moral principles that still constitute the foundation of idealism and spiritualism.

Good words strengthen the character, sweeten the heart and enlighten one's life. Bad words deaden the sentiments, pervert the behavior and kill the higher ideals.

Believing, wanting and talking rightly produce vibrations of peace that foster health, which changes one's emotional behavior. This, in turn, restores the balance of energy, altering the areas where illnesses might otherwise take hold.

Believing, wanting and talking rightly are infallible paths to a healthy existence.

Next, it is time for action, that is, for *operating rightly*.

The first three requisites reach their climax in action, without which they cease to influence the behavior that portrays one's inner reality.

Rightness is necessary at every step of human life.

A tranquil heart is the result of right conduct and, consequently, a fundamental factor for a peaceful conscience.

Therefore, these elements all depend on each other for one to live a happy life, since the ennobled sentiments enable one to look back without remorse and act without fear. This produces an imperturbable state of peace, for it is rooted in one's way of operating, leading one to walk rightly.

The world has always progressed, thanks to those who act uprightly. Past examples of their dedication to worthy causes have become the basis for the enhancement of life and other people.

Conscious of their responsibilities, they did not fear persecution, harsh struggles, sacrifices, and even death when necessary, if it meant that their ideal would remain pure. They knew that the death of the body cannot destroy a grand idea, and that it is in the blood of the martyr that the seed of truth germinates in order to sprout and grow at a later time, producing a blessing of blossoms and fruit.

Since the greatness or smallness of individuals is measured by their ideals, it is by their actions that the excellence of their aspirations is evaluated, because it is there, in the living of them, in the bringing of them to the objective world, that they must endure the intense heat of the forges into which they are thrown before they become reality.

Operating rightly is a real challenge when living among sickly individuals and in an unjust society. Senselessness escalates; well-woven conspiracies, hidden under a cloak of legality, swarm all round; moral concessions and connivance are regarded as almost normal. All these make correct action very difficult. Those who act uprightly seem to be mentally alienated; they are frowned on and are regarded as eccentric or as attention getters. In order to prevent the unmasking of fraud and corruption in predominance, there is an age-old, systematic opposition orchestrated against acting uprightly.

Operating rightly is both a preventative therapy and a cure for suffering.

Those who do not act wrongly do not have to repeat the experience, retrace their steps, or pay back debts...

Such action, however, begins with small decisions, the simplest, seemingly most unimportant tasks.

But everything in life is important. Small acts lay the groundwork for grand gestures and remarkable achievements.

Maintaining the same level of right conduct in a small matter as in a bigger one is training for a balanced experience.

Living rightly is, therefore, the next step.

The actions that follow one another first become individuals' *modus operandi,* and then become their *modus vivendi.*

Those who act rightly, live rightly.

Their today depicts their previous actions and their tomorrow will be the result of their present ones.

They do not hide in error; they do not get overexcited or depressed.

Their hours elapse harmoniously and their struggles, even when exhaustive, do not make them unhappy, because they are means for reaching the higher levels that await them.

Life expands infinitely, since it does not end with the grave; hence it acquires meaning and significance, and is filled with excellent opportunities for learning and fulfillment.

Gandhi put forth racial equality, and equal rights and duties. However, for his ideals to be truly respected, he lived accordingly, working at the loom and welcoming pariahs at his ashram, granting them the same consideration as any other person.

He lived frugally, according to what he considered the basic necessities of life, and he advised others to do the same.

As we stated earlier, Jesus did not have a stone on which to lay His head, even though the birds in the sky had their nests, and the beasts their dens, because for Him only one thing was important: *giving of Himself* in a world of things that are worth only what is attributed to them, for they have no intrinsic value...

Such a life requires a great effort because *wide is the door that leads to destruction.*

The next step is to put forth the correct effort.

Without effort, no endeavor is possible, much less successful.

Intensity of effort reveals quality of character.

Without discipline strengthened by exertion, effort vanishes and aspirations die.

The power of effort, which derives from wanting, is responsible for the outcomes of aspirations put in practice.

People who do not strive to preserve their grand ideals lose the battles of evolution before they even engage them, upsetting the march of general progress.

As a justification for not making an effort, it is often said that it is not possible to maintain the optimal level of one's ideals. However, the practice of bad habits occurs through efforts naturally incorporated into everyday life.

Breaking them is possible only by employing energies that oppose them.

Frequently, due to the pleasure of their addictions, individuals make enormous sacrifices and use every means conceivable to continue the enslaving sensations. However, if anyone suggests a *change* to long-term fulfillment, they refuse to make the effort because they are comfortable as is, even if it is ruining their lives.

Nobody can live effortlessly. Beyond the limits of its automatic phenomena, life requires the use of the will and the focusing of energies.

Those who make an effort in one area can do so in another, if they wish.

Putting forth the correct effort means knowing how to use one's resources for what provides real, lasting happiness, without the woes of fleeting pleasures, which have to be repeated endlessly because they do not quench one's thirst but only make it worse.

In a well-directed effort, one's energies are reinvigorated and one's motivations – since they are of a higher nature – attract new endeavors that surpass one's limitations and the stress of suffering.

The mind, fixed at a higher level, numbs the sensations of imbalances and infirmities, and emulates the acquisition of harmony, which is achieved through rightly applied effort.

Making small and constant attempts to act correctly develops forces that will be channeled toward grand commitments, even if unknown to other people.

Continuous moral renewal and all the work of changing one's behavior require the right kind of effort that leads to success. Being inward in character, they derive from the belief in one's goals and their inherent value so as to resolutely want them and invest in the effort to reach them; otherwise, the endeavor will fail.

This effort stems from the application of *thinking rightly.*

What is cultivated in one's thinking spills over into the objective realm and becomes an existential element in one's behavior.

Thought is a generating source and a conducting dynamo from Life to life.

Energy is present everywhere, waiting for thought to command and direct it.

With regard to the many aspects of suffering, mental activity is highly important.

All those who allow themselves to be led by pessimism and depression create morbid states and get caught in the webs of entirely avoidable pain. By a process of natural affinity, they tune into illnesses and open gaps in their immunity for the onset of afflicting ailments and disorders. The constant bombardment against the delicate mechanisms of the emotions and the physical body ends up disrupting their harmony, thereby producing imbalances that facilitate the entry of degenerative agents.

Thinking rightly, by contrast, strengthens the psychophysical field, expelling illnesses and generating successive waves of well-being, which are responsible for one's health.

Added to all this is the interference of discarnate spirits in people's daily lives.

Mental emissions sent in one direction or another foster attunement with spirits of a corresponding energy pattern. Thus, one cannot be surprised at the current epidemic of obsessions, stemming from the mental and moral affinity existing between perturbed individuals and the unhappy spirits with whom the former maintain an ideological coexistence.

Sickly ideoplasties – bizarre and unhealthy thought-forms – end up creating a toxic psychosphere that poisons people, increasing the numbers of diseases that are hard to diagnose using conventional medicine. In such cases, patients will have to treat themselves by means of a radical change in mental and moral behavior in order to break free of the enveloping vibrations.

Thinking rightly promotes psychological harmony and attunement with the Spirit benefactors of humankind. On contact with them, individuals draw health-supporting energy, which will act on the causes of sufferings, altering their duration and effects.

Those who think rightly find themselves, others, and God.

The sound habit of thinking leads to the final stage, which is *meditating rightly*.

Fixed on the panels of the memory, due to a pernicious mental education, are a huge number of unhappy scenes, reproachable acts and inferior aspirations, and that is why meditation is brushed aside as being too hard.

However, all one has to do is to change the direction of one's mental habits and the foundations for meditation can be laid.

Since no one can live without thinking – except for bearers of severe psychopathologies – one always ought to think positively and optimistically. This will begin generating a new habit in the mental field until it is assimilated and transformed into an automatism through natural repetition.

Out of bad habit, when something bad happens, people let themselves be consumed by it. They give in to it, comment on it, repeat it and give it roots, whereas the right course of action is the complete opposite. But when something good and useful happens, they seldom analyze, internalize and relive it. Instead, they replace it with something else that is unpleasant, holding on to the latter in detriment of the former. It is only natural that, unaccustomed to reflecting on goodness, peace, health and joy, people find it difficult to meditate rightly.

In the first attempts, archived memories release depressing, pernicious scenes and candidates just give up. What they should do instead is put forth the effort to break free of them by imprinting new images and aspirations that generate health and happiness.

Concentration entails focusing the mind, due to interest or selection, on some thought or special idea that one desires to examine or retain.

Meditation is the use of concentration in the inner search for God with determination and perseverance. Its only goal is to experience the Divine Flow and know God, sense Him and feed on His energy. It is the state of mental stillness.

Jesus said, *"Your eye is the light of your body. If your eye is one, your whole body will be illumined."*

If individuals will allow themselves to look within, they will have one, single visual idea; in capturing the Divine Light, their entire being will also become illumined. Consequently, no suffering will perturb them, thanks to the acquisition of complete health.

Meditation replenishes wholesome energies, restoring the harmony of one's psyche; and the psyche restores the harmony of the physical body.

Those who meditate believe, want, talk, operate, live, strive and think rightly, acquiring the values necessary for salvation. At this stage, they surrender and no longer live: it is *Christ who lives in them.*

They are released from suffering at last.

Sufferings due to prior causes are frequently, like those that arise from current wrongs, the natural consequence of wrongs that were committed previously; that is, through justice that is strictly meted out, humans bear what they made others bear.

Sufferings due to prior causes are frequently, like those that arise from current wrongs, the natural consequence of wrongs that were committed previously; that is, through justice that is strictly meted out, humans bear what they made others bear.

KARDEC, Allan – *The Gospel according to Spiritism*, Chap. V, no. 7 (1st ed., ISC.)

9

THE PROCESS
OF SELF-HEALING

Human beings possess invaluable, untapped resources just waiting to be channeled appropriately. Among them, bioenergy[5] is a source of inexhaustible potential misused out of ignorance and neglect, unconsciously squandering precious forces.

Invisible to ordinary optics, bioenergetic radiation goes unnoticed as it exerts its influence on inter-personal relationships, provoking either waves of affinity or animosity, depending on whether they proceed from a morally healthy or morally sick individual.

Absorbed by the perispirit[6], bioenergy acts upon it by way of its own field, renewing or perturbing the perispirit's forces, according to the type of discharge.

Bioenergy is responsible for interpersonal attraction, paralleling the attraction that happens in the molecular, cellular, gravitational and universal fields.

Similar to the invisible magnetic field that surrounds the earth, and which is only detected by special equipment, bioenergy is also perceived only through paranormal means or ultra-high speed cameras using ultrasensitive film.

---

[5]   Life energy – Tr.
[6]   Kardec's terminology for what is also known as the astral body – Tr.

Its influence, however, is very easily detected in the emotions, in areas affected by infirmities due to the psychological reactions they provoke in human relationships.

Referring to the phenomena bioenergy produces, Jesus, the Ultimate Healer, was peremptory in saying: *"You can do greater things than these"* if you want to.

That *want to* is extremely important since it represents not only the interested, immediate will, but the effort and investment of resources for taking full command of that force and skillfully channeling it for higher purposes.

The purpose of its application is also important. All those who use it for worthless ends or for fun become victims of their own imbalance, and they will suffer the harmful effects of its misuse.

On the other hand, practicing the proper application of bioenergy develops the range of its beneficial action, rendering it an invaluable healing resource of inestimable significance.

It can be directed through prayer, concentration, meditation and good sentiments to benefit others and oneself, utilizing it for the recovery of one's health, peace and well-being, and for high-minded goals.

The results will not be immediate, of course, but they will come in due time. Since suffering is a need for debtor spirits, being freed from it depends on several duly-observed prerequisites, some of which have already been analyzed.

Nevertheless, God's love, through *His superlative mercy,* provides debtors with the opportunity to experience balance in order to motivate them to work for its full acquisition.

Thus, in light of suffering, particularly suffering as the result of infirmities, a number of factors should be taken into consideration to effect self-healing. By extension, one may also apply them on behalf of other ailing people when necessary.

1) OBSERVING ONE'S THOUGHTS AND THEIR PREFERRED CONTENT IN ORDER TO RADIATE POSITIVE, HEALTHY ENERGY.

The immediate attitude to have is to *fervently desire health,* and not to merely be free from illness.

If release from an illness does not engage the patient in positive mental and physical activities, it will open the door for other illnesses.

The yearning for health must be accompanied by uplifting, achievable goals and not by the immediate interest for the pleasures one wants to enjoy. That would discharge waves of negative energy into the intricate perispiritual components responsible for the outcome.

This desire for health is grounded in the belief and certainty that the *Father does not want the destruction of the sinner, but of the sin,* and those who defraud the law must make amends.

The firmness of the desire, without anxiety or torment – so that it does not become a demand but a request – brings tranquility to the ailing person, which is the first step toward a cure.

Then, one should *concentrate on health,* reflecting on its worth and the abundance of constructive possibilities, productive achievements and beneficial effects it provides for oneself and society.

When concentrating on it, one should surrender one's body and soul to the forthcoming results, allowing oneself to be infused with optimism and an unreserved trust in God, working mentally for the restoration of debilitated forces in a continuous effort aimed at well-being.

Irritation, anxiety, discontent, jealousy and rebelliousness must be rejected whenever they try to sneak onto the mental landscape, for they bear a harmful radiation that disrupts the cellular centers, upsetting their rhythm and reproduction.

Ennobling ideas and plans for future beneficent activities are bearers of stabilizing energy, which stimulates the complex cellular fields, rendering them harmonious and productive.

In this effort, it is well-advised to *visualize health* and embody it.

One should focus on a vision of health, projecting oneself forward in time experiencing equilibrium; one should see oneself as healed, assuming responsibilities and developing activities that one wishes to get involved in.

This mental projection restructures the dynamics of the affected perispirit and restores its field, which results in health, harmony and enthusiasm.

Of course there are exceptions, but patients usually visualize their illness worsening, and this shoots destructive mental projectiles into the body.

Many times, Jesus said to the infirm that came to Him: *If you want it, it is done*, and concluding: *Arise and walk, see, be cleansed*, depending on the infirmity.

At that very moment, the patient exited the vibrational field of darkness where he or she once hid, and became receptive to the Divine Benefactor's powerful energy, which altered the problem area, restoring it to health.

Thus, visualizing oneself as healthy in the future and then taking action to make it so are key factors for self-healing.

2) KEEPING MENTAL ATTUNEMENT WITH THE SOURCE OF POWER.

All love comes from God, the Source of Power. Consequently, the patient's mental attunement with that Causality is essential for regaining health.

Since infirmity is the result of vibratory disharmony in the body's organs, allowing for the proliferation of destructive elements, healing efforts must be aimed at balancing the energy field primarily, which in turn will recompose the denser structures of the body. Otherwise stated, healing follows the spirit /matter sequence.

Thus, a patient's mental oneness with the Generating Source of Life is essential for reestablishing harmony.

Hence, the cultivation of positive ideas leads to oneness with higher vibratory bandwidths, which produces the necessary attunement with the Supreme Power.

Prayer is another means for mental attunement with God. It fosters an analysis of one's needs in relation to the essential purposes of existence. At the same time, it promotes the relaxation of tensions, stimulating and renewing weakened forces, which, in turn, opens the way to the recovery of health.

Accustomed to impure thoughts and acting under impulses of depression or violence, individuals poison themselves with toxic energy, which further perturbs and sickens them.

Changing one's mental focus and instilling healthy ideas generates a harmonious psychosphere that produces conditions propitious for well-being. It is a first step toward attunement with health.

Those who breathe pure oxygen detoxify quicker, expanding their breathing capacity. Likewise, mental attunement with the Source of Power helps reestablish healthy energy, which then reinstates the body's lost equilibrium. This in turn restores vibrational harmony, fostering the predominance of the agents of health.

Even in light of an apparently delayed recovery, one must continue to strive for attunement, which will provide emotional, psychological and organic benefits.

One must lift oneself up to God, not just to ask for immediate benefits, but also to stay in harmony with life itself.

Such a state of attunement opens the doors of one's extra-physical perception to inspiration, balance and the courage to face any foreseen or unforeseen disturbing events and situations.

When one uplifts him or herself to God, all humanity is uplifted.

Attunement with God, the Source of Power, is the cause of happiness and an agent of peace.

3) RESTING, A HEALTHY DIET, HYGIENE AND KEEPING ACTIVITIES IN ORDER.

Physical rest is highly important for self-healing; however, mental rest, which results from harmonious thoughts, is absolutely vital – a must for regaining one's health.

A mind at rest does not imply idleness but positive action that generates balance. This in turn provides rest from perturbing agitation, emotions and feelings responsible for illness and suffering.

Uplifting and optimistic literature, rich with hope, provides mental and physical relaxation, predisposing the body to tranquility and harmony.

Such rest may also be achieved by way of a well-balanced diet that avoids excesses, especially foods that are high in calories or are hard to digest and assimilate.

The correct approach entails eating to live, respecting the limits imposed by one's infirmity, instead of living to eat, which complicates the functions of an already debilitated body that needs all of its resistance to recover.

Hygiene also plays a major role in regaining one's health. It helps in the elimination of toxins while providing a pleasant sensation of lightness.

Physical hygiene also requires mental hygiene, whose content, if polluted by pernicious preferences, causes the breakdown of the body's inner workings, like rust in mechanical parts that must work harmoniously.

These factors bring order to activities unaffected by illness, or to those that, despite the health problem, deserve consideration and planning for later implementation.

Those who fail to plan suffer the surprises derived from a lack of foresight and any damage that might result from it.

The sickbed is the place for profound meditation and goal setting, which the daily grind does not otherwise allow for. At the same time, a review of one's acts and behaviors is timely, in that one can seek to uncover the origin of some of one's current ills or the effects of the thoughtless actions that have caused them.

Organic degeneration is quick and easy, whereas recovery is complex and time consuming. Building and rebuilding takes time and experience, which is not the case with destructive action.

A healthy life, therefore, is the product of concentrated efforts for the maintenance of the body's components under the balanced command of the spirit.

Of course there are healthy and apparently harmonious bodies under the direction of frivolous, ignorant and even perverse spirits. This is a natural occurrence, which will reach a regrettable level in the future due to the present-day abuse, requiring a slow and painful recovery through harrowing, painful infirmities.

According to Divine Law, nobody can abuse the gift of life without suffering dire consequences.

Likewise, one frequently finds suffering, disabled bodies indwelt by joyful, healthy spirits. They are the masters of selflessness who rise above their organic handicap to teach courage in the face of pain, and to atone for old debts recorded on the pages of time and which now resurface to offer complete liberation.

In all Creation the *Law of Equality* is in force, according to which no one enjoys happiness by exception. Struggle is the common denominator for all beings on the path of evolution.

4) CHANNELING ONE'S THOUGHTS AND EMOTIONS TOWARD LOVE, COMPASSION, JUSTICE, EQUANIMITY AND PEACE.

Optimistic thinking predisposes one to an emotional state receptive to health. Thus it is easy to channel it toward the ennobling expressions of love, compassion, justice, equanimity and peace.

The magic élan that will unite all people someday, love must be cultivated as a new experience, the practice of which will become a habit, a normal state of the spirit.

Love's power restores one's confidence in people and in life, for its presence produces stimuli that enable the blood to periodically receive revitalizing charges of adrenaline that reinvigorate the body.

Through its optics, events reveal previously unseen aspects, keeping the emotions from becoming either deadened or overexcited, while at the same time predisposing one to the humanizing quality of compassion.

When the combined forces of fear and anger, bitterness and revenge, jealousy and hatred begin to perturb the emotions, the sentiment of compassion for the tormenter, presenting him or her as fragile and vulnerable, prevents imbalance from turning into aggression on the part of the victim. The victim then sees the opponent as a sickly soul unaware of the gravity of his or her own wrong, and instead of becoming hostile, the victim envelops the tormenter in waves of sympathy and understanding, thus avoiding returning a wrong for a wrong.

Within the framework of the ills that afflict humans, we find lodged in the perispirit various matrices of hatred, resentment and bitterness toward other people.

Love offers the compassion that one would like to receive if the situation were reversed; it decreases the intensity of the blow and nullifies its harmful effects. Compassion speaks of God's Inexorable Justice, which reaches everyone and requires benevolence toward one's opponent, rendering him or her – albeit indirectly – aware of the fact that a wrong is always worse for the one who commits it.

Justice, in turn, is already engraved on each person's conscience, and although it may be anesthetized for some time, it can never be completely suppressed.

Wrongdoers know their error, and they try to hide it because they know its origin.

Merely covering up a wound does not keep it from infecting the surrounding area.

Justice in the conscience demands reparation for the offense and its unfortunate consequences, inducing victims not to act as debt collectors since the sovereign laws have the means to prevent new debts when old ones are being paid.

To achieve its purposes, justice has to be based on equanimity, which discerns how to apply it without the emotional contribution of passion of any kind, but with the higher purpose of correcting without retaliation, and redeeming without abuse.

The sentiment of equanimity comes from reason, which discerns, and emotion, which understands, assuring that the means and the methods of reeducation are the same for all subjected to its codes; it is neither too severe for some, nor overly benevolent for others. Its straight line of action grants equal treatment to all offenders.

The mindfulness of love with equanimity proposes peace, which removes all tensions and inspires further action. An inner state of harmony, it radiates outward in successive waves of tranquility, promoting the body's absorption and assimilation of healthy energies.

Thought channeled toward peace becomes a wave that synchronizes with the Source of Power, contributing to general understanding and fraternity, which is the first step of love between individuals.

During the self-healing process, the spirit recoups spent energies and uses thought to vitalize its perispiritual centers, predisposing it to redemption through love. It does not negotiate benefits, but desires to be useful to society, an active member of overall progress instead of an unhappy, unpleasant weight on the social economy.

The coauthor of its own recovery, the spirit draws wholesome energies from the providential Source of God's love, leaving the darkness of infirmity for the light of health, willing to contribute decisively to a better world today and tomorrow, renewed, enlightened and happy.

The means of combating obsession vary depending on the characteristics in which it appears... (No. 249)

The moral imperfections of those who are obsessed are frequently an obstacle to their liberation... (No. 252)

Furthermore, the ascendancy that humans can have over spirits is in proportion to their superior moral development. They cannot dominate highly evolved spirits, or even those who, without being so evolved, are nevertheless good and benevolent. However, they can dominate spirits who are of low moral development. (No. 254)

KARDEC, Allan – *The Mediums' Book*, Chap. XXIII
(1st ed., ISC)

10
DISOBSESSION THERAPY[7]

In the study of human suffering one chapter stands out, which, due to its severe implications, deserves to be studied separately.

A moral blight of the spirit, obsession is much more widespread than one might imagine, periodically becoming a swiftly contagious *virus* by virtue of circumstances, which, as a consequence of the evolution of the individual and the planet, require the cleansing of a huge amount of bad debt still weighing on the social economy.

In Eastern antiquity, and later during the Middle Ages, obsession took on epidemic proportions, sweeping nations, giving them a reprieve, and then returning unexpectedly.

Confused with insanity in its many forms, obsession has challenged scholars of behavior, health, religion and mental science.

It is usually subtle, but at times it assumes unexpected proportions, leading those who fall into its grip to unfortunate extremes.

---

[7] It entails a dialogue to enlighten discarnate spirits who exert a harmful influence on incarnate individuals. For more in-depth information please see paragraph 249 of *The Mediums' Book* by Allan Kardec – Tr.

Humanity has suffered its effects, periodically considering it a *divine punishment*. The methods used to combat it have been no less cruel due to ignorance about its origin, making it impossible to confront and ameliorate it using skillful, effective means.

This is insanity by reason of obsession, that is, by reason of the interference of the mental presence of a discarnate spirit in the life of an incarnate spirit.

Obsession can also malevolently influence the physical organization, producing pathologies as complex as they are harmful.

Allan Kardec studied it proficiently and was the first investigator to penetrate its causes and dissect them, presenting compatible therapies capable of minimizing or eradicating it altogether.

Before Kardec, Jesus repeatedly faced and assisted obsessors and the obsessed with His ineffable love, freeing them from each other with His restorative power.

His dialogs with these sickly individuals are profound, and they offer a remarkable field of study to psychopathology, which is still in the dark as far as specialized subjects are concerned.

However, by dealing with the causal factors, Spiritism analyzes and explains the problem, proposes proper methods for helping those involved, and provides preventative therapies to keep the illness from taking hold.

Obsession has its roots in the moral past of both complainants, who allowed themselves to be defeated by the inferiority that dominated them at the time of their skirmish.

Selfish and thoughtless, they did not measure the consequences of their venal acts, and became bound to each other with shackles of hatred and revenge that made them increasingly miserable.

Consequently, they plod along for centuries of excruciating suffering, switching back and forth from victim to tormenter, until love kindles the light of hope in their darkness, and forgiveness makes them true siblings on the evolutionary path.

Love, therefore, is the first medication to be used in disobsession therapy.

Love opens the doors to hope and reveals the sacred purposes of life, enabling forgiveness to soothe the pain caused by the ulcerations of hatred. As long as resentment, ill-will, distrust and spite persist, obsession is an acid burning the delicate mental components and producing tormenting mental problems.

Mediumship, on the other hand, is the grand opportunity that identifies and cures obsession, because it is through its intricate mechanisms that obsessions manifest, and the parties can be addressed.

The patient, the victim of obsession, is certainly endowed with mediumship, and he or she needs the proper education to apply it constructively.

Obsession is a severe *disease,* even when it appears in the simple form of a depressive inspiration or a *pathological state* that compromises physical health. This is because it requires the patient's moral transformation and an emotional shift on the part of the obsessor who, conscious of it or not, has set it in motion.

Obsession exists only because the obsessed person owes a moral debt.

The laws of life have wonderful means for reeducating those who violate their codes of justice. However, individuals' intemperance and hastiness, along with their own disturbances, lead them to retaliation and revenge, producing these unnecessary experiences of suffering.

The unhappy mind, set solely on revenge, shoots waves of hatred at its enemy, who, lacking moral resources such as watchfulness, charity and love, registers them through the perispirit on account of mutual, vibratory affinity, until such waves become a perturbing idea in the victim's psyche.

At other times, the obsessor spirit emits the same deleterious energies and uses its will to condense its vibrations to manifest in terrifying apparitions during the waking state and the partial disengagement of sleep, establishing a connection through sheer horror that develops into the pathology of hallucination.

With successive interferences, the obsessor finally dominates the guilty mind, which becomes submissive, giving rein to the gravest phenomena of subjugation, which, for centuries, ignorance has considered as being demonic possession and science has labeled as schizophrenia.

Similarly, the constant *psychic ingestion* of the sickly mental wave produces various organic disorders, which either enable destructive germs to set in, or directly cause cellular degeneration, ulceration and dysfunction in various organs.

Disobsession, therefore, is a specialized therapy and it alone has the resources for setting the mentally alienated free.

By enlightening the infirm spirit imbued with a wrongful notion of justice, one must dissuade it from its purpose, showing it its error and leading it to the certainty that God's love solves everything.

Upon completion of this task, which requires the participation of an educated medium if psychophony[8] does not occur through the actual patient, it is essential to inform the victim about his or her situation. He or she can then seek rehabilitation by means of a change in mental and spiritual behavior, using the techniques referred to in the chapter on self-healing.

This moral reform of the obsessed person will cause the obsessor to appreciate his or her efforts to improve, demonstrating regret for past actions, such that the two can become friends and advance together on the path of the good.

The ministry of disobsession can also take place beyond the physical realm. Spirit benefactors may intercede when they see the victim-soul's effort to rehabilitate itself and help its persecutor.

Regarding obsessions that affect the physical body, besides using liberating, spiritual therapy, corresponding medical therapy is also appropriate for physical recovery.

Obsessions also proliferate between incarnates as the result of abuses of the sentiments. These abuses lead to psychic vampirization, generating long-lasting disorders.

Perturbing desires shoot mental darts that strike their target, causing strange and unpleasant sensations. When reciprocal, they give course to psychic interdependence, producing suffering by affecting the emotions as well as the body.

Every form of obsession results from an interpersonal relationship disrupted by the negative forces of aggression, hatred, betrayal, crime or misguided expressions of love, which throw the sentiments into disarray.

---

8 Oral communication by spirits through mediums – Tr.

Disobsession entails interrupting the magnetization between both wretches, for the obsessor spirit, despite considering itself satisfied due to the harm it inflicts on its victim, also suffers from its own misery and lack of peace.

People are always responsible for their own lives. There is sorrow, obsession and suffering only when they choose unhealthy instead of healthy behaviors.

Obsession indicates a re-emergence of unfortunate acts in search of immediate reparation.

Dissolving the fetters of evil with the powerful energy of love during disobsession therapy thus releases individuals from the suffering caused by their negligence and blesses them with complete health, which is the result of a mind in harmony with life, a physical organization in balance, and emotions and reason aimed at the good, progress and happiness.

*If physicians fail in treating most ailments,
it is because they treat the body without treating
the soul, and since the whole is not in a good state,
it is impossible for any one part of it to be well.*

KARDEC, Allan – *The Gospel according to Spiritism*
Introduction – Section XIX
Summary of the Doctrine of Socrates and Plato (1st ed., ISC.)

11
ALTERNATIVE THERAPIES

Ignorance is largely responsible for suffering, for it generates selfishness, which in turn fosters attachment to and passion for people and things.

Considering the impermanence of everything in a world of constant change, attachment is an illusion for halting the march of events and putting everything else on hold, preventing the emergence of reality.

The impermanent is the transitory materialization of reality; consequently, any over-attachment to form produces suffering on account of the inevitable changes it undergoes. This is analogous to trying to stop time, which is an illusion that will only frustrate anyone attempting it.

Thus, most infirmities originate in the emotions as a result of an energy imbalance that spills over into the mental or physical arena, harming the organic structure.

The therapies of classic medicine almost always focus on sustaining the body by stopping illnesses and destroying *harmful invaders.*

With minor methodological variations, all Western medical philosophy is focused on that goal as being essential to health.

In contrast, Eastern wisdom has held for millennia that, since illnesses are the result of disruptions of energy – due to causes examined in previous chapters – they must be combated at their roots.

Thus, there are various alternative techniques for acquiring health by abolishing such causes.

These therapies are now appearing in the West, making way for eliminating or at least modifying suffering by restoring the person's balance of energy.

Spiritist Science, in turn, recognizes that all suffering stems from the misuse of free will; therefore, the key to ending suffering is the individual's moral regeneration.

This thesis extends to the problem of illnesses.

Without a corresponding moral change, any therapy used may modify the patient's physical condition but not heal it, because at the first opportunity the illness will return or foster the manifestation of other pathologies already existing in a still-unbalanced vibratory field.

Alternative therapies are essentially concerned with the whole person, with the entire complex that externalizes in the body and not just the body per se.

Acupuncture, for example, regards the body as an instrument of an *energy system* and is thus non-physical, that is, less dense than it appears to be. This system prevails over the whole as if it were another, more complex nervous system sustaining all the delicate workings and the most subtle implements of the somatic organization. It maintains the mind/body, emotion/sensation and thought/matter interaction.

Acupuncture seeks to use the physical body to reach this energy field and vitalize it, eliminating blockages that impede irrigation by health-supporting forces.

This energy system is made up of *meridians*, which are currents of energy running throughout the entire body.

It is relatively easy to find and measure the energy-charged acupuncture points along the meridians. The tobiscope, a highly sensitive electric apparatus, can locate them, thus proving their existence.

It is believed that there are fourteen main meridians and fifty-seven secondary ones constituting the energy system.

If there is any blockage in the energy flow or any imbalance resulting from a destructive mental force and reproachable moral acts, infirmities take root. Applying needles at the acupuncture points rebalances the energy of the meridian and unblocks it; the generator system is rebuilt and health is restored.

These sensitive points can even provide anesthesia for critical surgical treatments, births, etc.

Another practice of inestimable value is yoga, especially for imbalanced emotions, serious psychological problems, and a few other health issues.

Knowledge of the *chakras* (wheels) as sources of energy in the body's vitalizing system has provided techniques for the development, nourishment and balance of forces for maintaining the physical body, which the spirit uses in the process of evolution.

The chakras, traditionally seven in number, are considered to be *organs of energy*.

From the *crown* chakra down to the *root* chakra, they support the body's mental and physiological functions.

According to the same tradition, the most important thing about the chakras is what is called the *Kundalini energy*, also known as the *sleeping serpent*, which ascends up the spine, nourishing the chakras while being sustained by them. It is also responsible for energizing the nerves.

When dormant at the base, it automatically tends to the organization of the chakras.

Through meditation, rhythmic exercises and various other techniques, the Kundalini is awakened and its energy can be channeled appropriately, attending to the chakras, expanding spiritual awareness and fostering physical health, vitality and the harmony of the nervous system.

Also called the *serpent of fire*, its energy can be applied to restore one's personal health, as well as that of other individuals.

Yoga fosters psychophysical balance and has become an invaluable form of alternative therapy.

Chromotherapy may have been inspired by *heliotherapy*, the latter consisting of the balanced use of the sun's rays, causing a salutary activation of the body's vital mechanisms.

For example, under the action of ultraviolet rays, 7-dehydrocholesterol turns into vitamin D, which prevents rickets.

Its results are excellent when, under careful control, the time of exposure to the sun is increased for treating spasmophilia, childhood anemia and asthma, various types of asthenia during convalescence, cutaneous tuberculosis, multiple dermatoses, etc.

Solariums have been shown to be effective against neuranemias, neurasthenias, etc.

Using colors, chromotherapy has led to some favorable results in the area of health, especially in cases of mental imbalance.

The color red is considered exciting, while blue is calming. Hence, red is used for melancholic states and blue for overly excitable ones, as in cases of delirium tremens and the like.

Chromotherapy properly applied through a correct knowledge of colors and their effects leads to recovery.

For example, red light produces good results in certain infectious states such as smallpox.

Homeopathy came into being around 1796, when Samuel Hahnemann began using it after publishing his *"Essay on a new principle for ascertaining the curative powers of drugs, with a few glances at those hitherto employed."*

He had tested the new therapy on himself and his family for six years, with remarkable results.

Homeopathy is based on the principle *similia similibus curantur*, that is, likes are cured by likes. Through infinitesimal dilutions, in which, theoretically, molecules of the original substance should no longer exist, the medication ceases to be chemical and becomes physical.

Since everything in the universe is energy and matter converting into each other, energy resources should be applied to rebalance the physical body, which, in its essence, also consists of the energy necessary for life.

Alternative therapies are multiplying: *psycho-biophysics, past life therapy, psychic and mediumistic surgeries, hypnosis, phytotherapy, flower therapy* and *crystal therapy*, among others, are working for the health and rebalancing of the individual, and the decline and even disappearance of suffering on the earth.

While acknowledging their invaluable contribution, we cannot forget that it is in the moral transformation of the individual for the better by means of charity – as prescribed by Spiritism and supported on the concept of Christ, who told those whom he healed *to stop sinning or something worse would happen to them,*[9] – that real healing occurs and suffering is mitigated, giving way to peace and psycho-physical balance.

[9]   Allusion to John 5:14 – Tr.

DEATH'S MESSENGERS

All they who thoughtless are, nor heed,
What time death's messengers appear,
Must long the pangs of suffering feel
In some base body habiting.
But all those good and holy men,
What time they see death's messengers,
Behave not thoughtless, but give heed
To what the Noble Doctrine says;
And in attachment frighted see
Of birth and death the fertile source,
And from attachment free themselves,
Thus birth and death extinguishing,
Secure and happy ones are they,
Released from all this fleeting show;
Exempted from all sin and fear,
All misery have they overcome.

Anguttara-Nikaya, III, 35
(www.sacred-texts.com/bud/bits/bits051.htm)

12
SUFFERING IN THE FACE OF DEATH

The impermanence of all things and people in the physical world is another cause of suffering.

Its duration results from the intensity of the causes that have engendered it.

In the case of illnesses, once the purifying trial or expiation has ended, the affected energy field is recomposed, fostering balance. However, in mental suffering, when the disharmony is emotional, individuals can use self-control, prayer, meditation and charitable actions to more easily free themselves from suffering, because they stop putting so much value on afflictions and see them instead as part of the natural process of evolution and, therefore, acceptable.

The acceptance of suffering is the decisive step for release from it, whereas rebelliousness has the exact opposite effect.

Once one understands that the body is a delicate organization subject to deterioration, wear, and then transformation through the phenomenon of death, one does not base the foundations of life or the essential realities on it. Thus, when disconnections and imbalances finally disrupt it for good, death does not become a reason for disgrace and ruin.

Appropriate preparation for facing death enables one to accept the fact that it is inevitable; thus suffering from it is mitigated.

When those who put all their hopes in the material life, seeing it as having only one aim, find that it is about to end, they experience superlative mental suffering, which turns into physical suffering with no immediate relief.

Thus, suffering has much to do with the psychological dispositions of each individual, the way he or she looks at life and its structure, at events and their origins.

Due to ignorance about life, death has been the cause of unimaginable suffering down through the millennia, triggering tragedies and endless woe.

Every biological phenomenon that begins naturally ceases; everything that is born on the physical plane is interrupted, transforms and, therefore, dies.

There is no time frame entailing absolute determinism. There can be innumerable reasons for the cycle to end... Hence, death is inevitable and the suffering it generates results solely from the misinterpretation of life's objectives.

Attachment to the decaying transitory form produces emotional distress, fostering the idea that everything has been consumed, and that nothing is left of what once was a human existence.

When all hopes are pinned on the body, the phenomena inherent to its constitution have a devastating impact on those who have identified with it.

In a way, this fact is the result of a materialistic cultural education, even under the spiritualist disguise. People join religious denominations without emotional bonding or a rational study of its content; consequently, death appears as the great destroyer of plans, aspirations and achievements.

By refusing to make a deep analysis of life, people go through their corporeal existence putting such a reflection off for a later time. They plan and enjoy life to the utmost under the conniving illusion of *carnal eternity*. When young, they postpone the examination of death to old age; when healthy, they wait until infirmity strikes, believing themselves invulnerable to wear and the degenerative phenomena of matter.

As time passes, they refuse to grow old, and they resort to surgery, physical fitness and nutrition in the vain attempt to hang on to their youth, unavoidably ravaged by the years. There is a tenacious struggle to conceal reality, and, when unsuccessful, neurotic crises and escape through alcohol, drugs or suicide may follow.

Thus, death has been blamed for occurrences that actually have nothing to do with it. People's own intemperance deserves the real credit.

Hence, the death of a loved one should not cause despair but joy, especially if he or she lived a praiseworthy existence.

The death of good persons and the continued life of bad ones are often deplored as being an aberration in the sovereign laws when, in fact, all is as it should be.

Because such good men and women were exemplary in their conduct and thought, they finished their commitments in the physical world and were able to return to their origin, whereas moral debtors, those of wrongful conduct, ought to be allowed more time for rehabilitation and rebalance.

Even when blessed with health, the body is a prison, and the liberation of a loved one who returns to plenitude should cause joy and not sorrow.

When bad people discarnate the same gladness should apply because death cut short their life of transgressions, perhaps giving them time to think, without amassing more debt or ruining themselves even further.

But in their stubbornness, that is not how people usually see it; they deny themselves a wholesome change of approach.

"I just can't believe it!" some exclaim. "What a tragedy!" say others. "I'll never accept it!" proclaim most people on the death of loved ones, hence willingly handing themselves over to suffering.

Unbridled pride and personal presumptuousness are their worst enemies in that they cloud their judgment in relation to what is a normal experience.

They see death everywhere but do not believe it will happen to them, at least for a while... A "while" that stretches out indefinitely in the sphere of their caprice.

Since death asks no questions, shocked relatives and friends surrender to emotional disarray and unnecessary, heartrending suffering.

Death always causes mixed feelings in those who leave, as well as in those who remain behind.

In any case it is normally a big surprise for everybody, and usually very unpleasant.

Those who have reflected on the event and prepared for it are quicker to adapt after the initial shock. However, for those who have made the body the center of all their attention, surprise is replaced by grief and unwarranted revolt, causing unsuspected ills.

The suffering deriving from death is therefore the result of the lens through which the mechanisms of life are observed.

Missing the deceased, grief, and concern about his or her situation in the afterlife are natural phenomena as a result of trials necessary for love, which must be sublimated due to the deceased's physical absence and all its implications.

Since true happiness cannot be experienced in the physical world, the day will come when one will experience it where there is no death, separation, or pain.

Thus, one must live, preparing to die and thinking about death so as not to suffer its afflictive injunction, avoiding desperation and its whole string of perturbing agents.

At the moment of death, everything appears confused at first. The soul needs some time to recognize itself; it feels dazed, like someone waking out of a deep sleep who tries to understand the situation. The lucidity of its ideas and the memory of its past returns as the influence of the matter from which it has just freed itself is extinguished and the sort of fog that had obscured its thoughts is dissipated.

The duration of the state of confusion following death varies greatly: it may last a few hours, several months or even years. The ones who experience it for the least amount of time are those who have identified themselves with their future state during life because they immediately understand their situation.

KARDEC, Allan − *The Spirits' Book*
Commentary to question no. 165
(4th ed., ISC)

13
SUFFERING
IN THE AFTERLIFE

In the light of Spiritism, the problem of suffering takes on a dimension unknown by most philosophical and religious doctrines, in that Spiritism amplifies its area of study and discussion.

Orthodox religions resolved the issue of Divine Justice through the application of eternal penalties and rewards. They established the concept of never-ending punishment, engendering a form of heavenly vengeance, in which love, compassion, benevolence, and justice itself are set aside and disregarded.

According to this criterion, offenders have no right to rehabilitation. Even when ignorant, psychopathic or simply rebellious, they are condemned without remission if they die in sin.

Severe at one moment, naïve the next, the same approach applies to fear-filled persons who repent, and to shrewd persons who claim to be submitting to dogma or accepting Christ as their savior, releasing them, as if by magic, from all suffering and blessing them with the everlasting happiness reserved for the righteous, as if unequal procedures merited equal qualification and reward.

Guilt marks the conscience like an open wound until a wrong is righted and the damaged energy field is recomposed. Sincere repentance or honest promises to change are not enough to rebalance the psyche and the emotions of offenders. Therefore, the more enlightened and lucid the transgressor, the greater his or her responsibility.

Wrongs hold their authors in their own web, which they must unmake by correcting what they did. This endeavor provides dignity and advances them.

Released from their wrongs, they gain experience and progress down the road in the direction of new levels of happiness, no longer held back by their past.

Not even their victims' forgiveness grants wrongdoers release from a guilty conscience. Of course, it does help offenders feel better about themselves and those they have harmed, which encourages them to repair the damage. Through love, and not hatred in the form of retaliation, the victory of moral recovery becomes more feasible, thereby delivering them from suffering.

Harbored while they are in the body, selfishness, the illusion of ownership and the presence of the primitive passions transfer the wounds they have caused into the afterlife.

Since humans are spirits, and the spirit is energy, their wrongs stay with them, producing maddening ulcerations wherever their spirit is, whether in the body or outside of it.

Death does not actually change anyone; it only changes individuals' position and vibratory situation, keeping them as they are.

It is natural that the "change of clothes" brought about by the end of the biological experience, does not extract the energy stratifications located in the seat of the conscience.

Discarnates awaken beyond the molecular vibrations of the body with the same skills, anxieties, illusions and cultivated necessities, whether good or bad, and assume a posture equivalent to the degree of their evolution.

The sensations predominant in their individuality remain. When they are backward, sensual, pleasure-loving and connected to sinister, licentious and selfish thoughts, they experience the same vibratory density that they were accustomed to while in the physical body. They *rematerialize* themselves and continue to live as if they were still incarcerated in the somatic body, suffering all its limitations, situations, conditionings, infirmities and wear... The mind, slave to sensations, creates ideoplastic forms that baffle them and make them despondent, making their suffering hard to describe.

They try to contact family members and friends left behind, but since these cannot perceive their presence, they feel afflicted with terrible anguish, leading them to insanity, violence and hopelessness.

At times, they rant and rave, and exhaust themselves, collapsing in paroxysms of despair until they faint, only to start again, over and over, until their darkened conscience receives the light of love, awakening them to a different type of suffering: remorse and repentance, which leads them to rebirth, to recovery under the stigmata of the cross engraved on their existence.

Until this help reaches them, they band together in groups of desperate spirits, who *construct* Dantesque regions, where they take refuge and continue under the incitement of punishments that the automatism of God's Law, inscribed within them as within all of us, imposes.

The suffering in these regions stems from assaults perpetrated with the consent of reason.

Nobody can evade the consequences of their actions, just as no plant can produce fruit different from its own fatalistic structure.

Love is the great Law of Life. Love establishes the criterion of justice with equality for all, as per the law of action and reaction.

The mental and moral conduct individuals cultivated while incarnate yields corresponding results, imbuing them with habits that translate into experiences of liberation or restraint, depending on their quality.

The continuation of life after physical death entails the same characteristics, the fixations resulting in future behavioral criteria. Because the addicted mind generates needs that cannot be satisfied there, suffering is constant for those who deceived themselves or harmed others.

When called to undergo purifying suffering, those imprisoned in ignorance about the Laws of Life often yield to rebelliousness and suicide to escape the coming *harvest*.

But to their absolute dismay, they encounter the life they reviled with their delirious gesture, adding to their new suffering the frustration of finding themselves indestructible, along with the afflictions deriving from the act itself. These afflictions produce lacerations in the perispirit, which begins suffering newfound ills. Besides these, which are part of their spiritual reality, there are other consequences such as: the grief or anger of family members; the negative act itself, which will encourage other people to defect in the future; the problems for those who remain behind – all cause suicides untold suffering, which can drag on for decades until it is time for them to return to earth bearing the marks of their desertion.

In other cases, some seek to escape degenerative diseases through euthanasia, with the naive idea of eternal sleep, whereas everything speaks of life, activity, progress.

The rest they seek is filled with gloomy nightmares and ruthless spirit beings, who inveigh against their act and torment them relentlessly.

Death by no means puts an end to suffering. Since it does not obliterate the psyche, it allows discarnates to reason and continue to participate in experiences; moreover, since perceptions belong to the spirit, these experiences continue to be transformed into sensations and emotions in the energy realm. Therefore, suffering corrects errors and leads offenders to make reparation.

No one should think of dying in order to be liberated, unless it is through the phenomenon of biological changes due to the process of death.

The illusion that individuals allow themselves, conceptualizing life as a biological accident, is largely responsible for the absurdities that cause them pain and suffering.

Only self-awareness and true individuation foster a healthy life on the earth and then beyond it, when the phenomenon of death occurs as a natural end to the biological cycle.

Since beyond the cadaverous disjunction individuals continue to be conscious of themselves, it is natural that their dominant sensations and emotions continue to affect them. In fact, those that were either a blessing or discord predominate even more vigorously with the continuation of life, though in another dimension.

In this panorama, the coarse sensations from which they did not want to be released or could not be released become even stronger, generating corresponding suffering, as if they were still in the physical realm.

In the area of the sentiments, as is understandable, cultivated fantasies and the imbalances of folly generate resentment, which is supplemented by complexes resulting from a guilty conscience on account of past wrongs, as well as everything positive they could have done but did not do.

A guilty conscience engenders mechanisms of repair that turn into nightmares of unnecessary repentance that act like a whip inflicting punishment.

Repentance must be an awakening to responsibility, which calls for reconstruction, renewal and reparative action without distress or misery.

Suffering in the afterlife also results in shocking conditions when, due to post-death perturbation, discarnates surrender to the ideoplasties of everyday life and *psychically construct* for themselves an *environment* and a *reality* that promote the continuance of the organic state with all its problems – though now in a different situation – prolonging the carnal illusion with all its perturbing ingredients, which are the result of the attachment to matter, from which death has not actually freed them.

Release from material conditionings is essential, disciplining the mind and the will in order to adapt immediately to the life beyond life. That is the only way suffering can be avoided, especially if the physical existence was characterized by ennobled actions, having achieved the main purpose of reincarnation – the pursuit of happiness.

An individual's moral and spiritual education is the sure means of deliverance from suffering on the earth, as well as beyond the grave, fostering a life abounding in peace.

*My brethren, take the prophets, who spoke
in the name of the Lord, as an example of
suffering and patience.*

*Indeed we count them blessed who endure. You
have heard of the perseverance of Job and seen
the intended by the Lord, that the Lord is very
compassionate and merciful.*

James 5:10-11

14

RELEASE FROM SUFFERING

Given the infinite range of suffering that afflicts human beings, the purpose of deep psychotherapy is to root out its causes.

In addition to the entire ethical and moral contribution that mitigates suffering and alters its causality, producing wholesome causes for the future, medical care, when dealing with issues in the area of physical health, and psychological care, when treating alienated behavior or personality conflicts, are extremely important.

Whatever the type of suffering, its claws cause wounds entailing a protracted degenerative process that sometimes leads to delusion, folly and arbitrariness, especially in individuals devoid of moral resistance.

Normally, its intensity is felt according to the sensitivity of those who experience it.

In the physical arena there are sufferers endowed with a high tolerance for pain, but who fail, disheartened, when the suffering is of an emotional nature.

The reverse is also true, consecrating heroes of almost unbelievable endurance under the yoke of terrible thorns embedded in the *tissues of the soul*.

Suffering is closely related to individuals' spiritual process.

Broad sensitivity endows them with greater emotional depth, which responds to anguish and inner conflicts without complaints or accusations. Sufferers silence their pain and let themselves be torn inwardly, especially when they experience emotional afflictions due to betrayal, injustice, cruelty, abandonment, loneliness...

If they have religious faith and transmute the trial for their spiritual future, they endure its cutting blades in a balanced way, overcoming the difficult situation and themselves, and exiting the crisis with greater maturity and peace. Lengthy illnesses beautify their character and endow them with even more loving feelings, which overflow with kindness.

When illnesses strike those who are less evolved, they brutalize them and harden the very core of their sentiments, which had been developing in a beneficial direction.

Because of its complex cultural, scientific, moral and religious structure, Spiritism is the Doctrine capable of solving the issue of suffering, setting its victims free.

Carl Gustav Jung was possibly the one who best probed into the reality of suffering, explaining it and offering a cure. While the general concern was about physical results and emotional well-being from the medical standpoint, Jung used two methods to find its cause and solution: dreams and the imagination.

Even though he admitted that a general approach in therapy is insufficient for offering assistance, since each case is specific and requires a special therapeutic language, he nevertheless adopted the two methods effectively with positive results.

At the same time, he recommended religious support, a source of outstanding contributions for the *healing of the soul*, where all causes of suffering originate.

Individuation and the journey toward the numinous were for him invaluable therapeutic dynamics for his patients' problems.

The moral advancement proposed by Spiritism, in addition to its extraordinary contribution in light of the fact that souls are immortal – heirs to their own acts, which, when misguided, cause suffering – and reincarnation – whereby spirits purify themselves, often through suffering – are irrefutable therapies for eliminating pain in humans and on the earth.

Suffering is temporary by being the effect of imbalanced energy, which, if directed toward the good and love, would no longer be disrupted, fostering enlightenment, plenitude, and therefore complete health, which the Father Creator has reserved for everyone in the world.

90337618R00090

Made in the USA
Columbia, SC
06 March 2018